Best Practices
21st Century Questioning & Problem Solving

Infolinking

Linda D. Ventriglia, Ph.D.

The Teaching Collection includes the following titles:

Best Practices Interdisciplinary Vocabulary Development
    The Rule of 3

Best Practices Differentiated Instruction
    The Rule of Foot

Best Practices Motivation and Student Engagement
    Creating Power Learners

Best Practices Interdisciplinary Literacy
    Stoplight Strategies

Best Practices for English Language Learning
    A Conversational Approach to Language and Literacy

Best Practices 21st Century Questioning and Problem Solving
    Infolinking

Best Practices for 21st Century Teaching
    The EduRevolution

Cover Design: Jesus Salcedo

8th edition
© 2009 by Linda D. Ventriglia, Ph.D.
ISBN 978-1-931277-02-0
Printed in Mexico

This book was printed in June 2009 at
Litográfica Ingramex, S.A. de C.V. Centeno 162-1,
Col. Granjas Esmeralda C.P. 09810, México, D.F.

Younglight
E D U C A T E
Light Up the Mind

The Younglight logo—a bright sun—represents lighting up the mind through learning. Younglight is committed to accelerating the achievement of all learners through professional development books that give teachers a repertoire of research-based Best Practices in teaching. By providing teachers with a repertoire of instructional strategies, Younglight carries out the promise of its logo, books that *Light Up the Mind.*

Visit www.younglighteducate.com
to find more educational titles in the
Best Practices series of books.

Preface to the Best Practices in Classroom Instruction Series

Quality Teaching: The Best Predictor of High Student Achievement

Student achievement is based on quality teaching. High quality teaching, along with stimulating interaction between students and teachers, ensures all students' academic success. This *Best Practices* classroom instruction series is based on the belief that teachers are the greatest resource available to students today.

Proven research-based *Best Practices* in this series provide teachers with a full repertoire of the instructional strategies needed to create optimal learning opportunities for diverse learners. These instructional strategies increase student achievement by focusing instruction on the content standards which are aligned with state assessments.

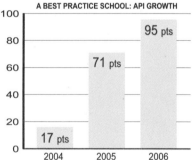

The Best Practice books and accompanying CD's are the result of ten years of school-based research. Schools that implemented the strategies outlined in the Best Practices in Classroom Instruction Series showed significantly greater gains in achievement than schools which were matched for socioeconomic status, percentage of free and reduced lunch, transience, attendance, student population and percentage of English learners. School wide adherence to Best Practices teaching—including differentiated instruction based on standards-based eight week benchmarks—resulted in dramatic gains in students' achievement. Academic improvement was palpable starting when the strategies were first employed, and gains continued year after year. Schools have achieved gold and distinguished status. Some teachers have become National Board certified.

Teachers using Best Practices reported that their classrooms were forever positively changed. Students became more engaged in learning. Best Practice teaching strategies challenged students to push the limits of their thinking to higher levels of problem solving. This changed the dynamics of learning in the classroom. Students became more thoughtful about what they were learning. They became more self motivated. As team leaders in cooperative groups, students mentored each other. The teacher's role changed from a director of learning to a facilitator of learning.

Best Practice teachers noted that after three years, the teaching strategies and classroom groupings became an integral part of how content was delivered and learned in their classrooms. Teachers at Best Practice schools established a learning community that went beyond their schools. The Best Practice concept of "teachers helping teachers" was implemented as teachers served as coaches and mentors of other teachers. This had a significant impact on teacher empowerment. It was the expertise of teachers reflecting on, modeling and implementing Best Practices that ultimately created success for all students.

Best Practices 21st Century Questioning and Problem Solving: Infolinking is the second book in the series. This book presents the importance of students learning to link information from multidisciplinary sources. The process of *infolinking,* connecting myriads of facts, is facilitated by the teacher who uses effective 21st century questioning across disciplines. There are many ways the teacher can structure questions both to increase factual knowledge and to extend students' thinking to higher levels. This book further discusses how students learn to ask their own strategic questions and to problem solve from multiple and multicultural perspectives.

Table of Contents

Chapter 1

Infolinking and 21st Century Learning

Twenty-first century learning does not focus on knowledge for knowledge's sake alone. It focuses on the linking of knowledge in new ways.

Content Organization in the Past, Present and Future

How does the Best Practice teacher transform the teaching and learning process for students who will spend their lives in the 21st century? How can the learning process become relevant for learners who live in a global age where change is the only constant? How can the learning process transcend the gap between the global interconnected world where students live and the disconnected way learning is currently delivered in most classrooms?

While educators neatly divide fields of study and make sure subject disciplines maintain their integrity, the rest of the global world—including businesses, professions, governments and trades—busily focuses on applying problem-solving skills and integrating knowledge across subject disciplines to get the job done.

Think about the organization of instruction in the majority of U.S. classrooms. Content is organized in specific disciplines. Mathematics is a separate area of knowledge from social studies, health and science. Elementary school instruction might focus on language arts and math in the morning and then move to social studies, health and science in the afternoon. If there is time music, art and health may be offered once a week. In middle school and high school, the segregation of subjects is even more defined. Students physically change classrooms to learn specific subjects. Specialty high schools go even farther in subject specialization. Although students at specialty schools take core topics, their electives are concentrated in health professions, science, music or performing arts.

While educators neatly divide fields of study and make sure subject disciplines maintain their integrity, the rest of the global world, including businesses, professions, governments and trades, busily focuses on applying problem-solving skills and integrating knowledge across subject disciplines to get the job done. In the health profession, medical researchers integrate knowledge and make connections from statistics, science, social science and global linguistics to figure out the cause and the influence of culture on diseases. Global businesses use statistics and probability and link facts taken from social science to try to figure out people's buying habits.

Companies, trades and professional communities are using information on the World Wide Web to address challenges and to create new understandings. They do not turn to a card catalog to find a book on the latest research. They use digital media to connect with sources of multidisciplinary information from around the world. Information is researched nonlinearly and applied creatively.

Global communication focuses on nonlinear information which is dynamic rather than static. The dissemination of digital information has fewer material constraints. Information can be rethought and reconfigured, and the space limitations that affect printed materials are almost eliminated. The only limiting factors are the storage space on a server, and the limitations imposed by reduced bandwidth. Other barriers to online access are falling due to wireless capabilities; Internet access doesn't require exclusive use of landlines as more and more remote areas of the world are connected via satellite communication.

On the information superhighway, facts can be linked and relinked. There are over 5 trillion keywords that can be used to find information. There are 500 billion links. There are also blogs and sites that video stream information. A topic may have over 1750 million linked words and 900 million linked articles, and a search on a web engine might list hundreds of thousands, if not millions of links.

Now think about the disconnection between how global businesses and professions access data and how students are taught to research information. Information is taught in concurrence with its definition as a noun. It is facts about a person, place or thing that is organized in a specific way. It can be found in a logical place, in a book, on a shelf, in a file or indexed in a card catalog. Each card represents one book or one isolated subject area. Students are taught that information in a file system or catalog is categorized in a specific manner (Wesch, 2008). Informational resources like the encyclopedia

On the information superhighway, facts can be linked and relinked. There are over 5 trillion keywords that can be used to find information. There are 500 billion links. There are also blogs and sites that video stream information. A topic may have over 1750 million linked words and 900 million linked articles, and a search on a web engine might list hundreds of thousands, if not millions of links.

are indexed with subjects strictly confined to alphabetical order. Sometimes there is cross referencing but oftentimes there is not. It requires a lot of effort for students to find information. Once the information is found, it is static. The linear text cannot be manipulated easily and unless the book is updated, the information can become dated.

Deep and Critical Thinking Through Infolinking

The nonlinear approach of organization challenges the basic principles of previous centuries' linear learning. Subject disciplines are categorized in response to an inquiry. There are a myriad of choices to explore any topic. Negotiation through this new informational landscape takes a new set of 21st century skills. What new skills do students need to possess in order to build upon their knowledge, problem solving abilities, innovation and creativity? Learning skills certainly require more than a basic knowledge of reading, writing and computing skills. The skills require more than memorizing specific discipline textual knowledge. They require students to ask questions, integrate knowledge and solve problems to create their own understandings.

The linking of combinations of facts to come up with new understandings and creative solutions to multidisciplinary challenges is termed *infolinking* **(Ventriglia, 2009). Infolinking is the 21st century process of transforming multidisciplinary facts by linking them together in new and creative ways.**

Twenty-first century learning does not focus on knowledge for knowledge's sake alone. It focuses on linking knowledge in new ways by asking challenging questions. The linking of combinations of facts to come up with new understandings and creative solutions to multidisciplinary challenges is termed *infolinking* (Ventriglia, 2009). Infolinking is the 21st century process of transforming multidisciplinary facts by linking them together in new and creative ways. Infolinking requires deep thinking and making critical choices on what information to connect and integrate. In order to practice 21st century infolinking successfully, students need to be taught two very important skills across subject areas. These critical skills are question asking and problem solving. The skills of question asking and problem solving are learned by students as teachers model higher level questions across disciplines. Then students must learn to formulate and ask their own questions. The formulation of inquiries to research a topic is a different and more difficult skill than responding to a teacher's questions.

After the questions are asked and information is found, then students need to problem solve to figure out how to link and apply the data to the solution of a problem. Similar to questioning, the skill of problem solving is learned best when it is applied across disciplines and in multicultural contexts. Problem solving can be taught in one subject discipline such as mathematics, but it eventually must be applied across various subject disciplines as well. It is the teacher's role as a facilitator of learning to expose students to the multidisciplinary applications of questioning and problem solving in the subject area or areas that he or she teaches.

There are many recent studies that confirm the value of infolinking as it ties to interdisciplinary and collaborative questioning and problem solving in the classroom. Teachers who encourage students to think deeply about subject areas and learn beyond the minimum amount of information help to break down the barriers of insulated subject areas and the academic/ vocational and arts/science divides. This helps students function successfully in the 21st century (Bereiter, 2005). Teachers who encourage dialogue between paired learners or cooperative groups facilitate the process of questioning and problem solving.

Bereiter and Scardamalia (2005) suggest that the purpose of teachers' encouraging "dialogic questioning" and the process of problem solving with a partner is to give students the opportunities to generate new knowledge and understandings. Students use dialogic questioning to build their own and each others' ideas by chaining or linking facts and concepts into coherent lines of thinking.

Bereiter and Scardamalia (2005) suggest that the purpose of teachers' encouraging "dialogic questioning" and the process of problem solving with a partner is to give students the opportunities to generate new knowledge and understandings. Students use dialogic questioning to build their own and each others' ideas by chaining or linking facts and concepts into coherent lines of thinking.

Working Together Across Disciplines to Solve Problems

In the book, *A Whole New Mind*, Daniel Pink (2006) reflects on how learning can be transcended in what he calls the Conceptual Age by having students work together to tackle novel challenges instead of routine problems. Students need to learn to synthesize and link information across disciplines to see the "big picture" rather than analyzing a single subject component.

Meizirow (2008) believes that students' learning is transformed by the teacher who takes them through the process of looking at the limitations of one-dimensional learning and instead shows them the advantages of considering multidimensional viewpoints and perspectives. He states that the process of transforming students' thinking begins as they become critically aware of how and why preconceived assumptions limit their thinking. This is the beginning of students using information from linked informational sources to create new understandings.

Creating new levels of understandings is one of the goals cited for 21st century learning in The Report and Mile Guide for 21st Century Skills. The report states:

Students now live in a multi-faceted, technology-driven world with almost unlimited streams of trivial and profound information, and myriad of choices. There are enormous opportunities to acquire knowledge in different ways and a myriad of multidisciplinary resources students can choose from. The goal of 21st century teaching is to help students integrate vital practical, emotional and social links across disciplines to make the best choices. (www.21stcenturyskills.org).

Saskatchewan (2005) states that the goal of 21st century learning and teaching must be to develop individuals who value knowledge and learning as a creative process. They must be able to construct strategic questions and creatively link informational sources to solve 21st century challenges.

> **Daniel Pink (2006) reflects on how learning can be transcended in what he calls the Conceptual Age by having students work together to tackle novel challenges instead of routine problems. Students need to learn to synthesize and link information across disciplines to see the "big picture" rather than analyzing a single subject component.**

Saskatchewan's statement is supported by the Standards for 21st Century Learners published by the American Association of School Librarians. These standards outline four important skills for 21st century learning:

1. Inquire, think critically and gain knowledge.

2. Draw conclusions, make informed decisions, apply knowledge to new situations, and create new knowledge.

3. Share knowledge and participate ethically and productively as members of our democratic society.

4. Pursue personal and aesthetic growth (American Association of School Librarians, 2008).

The importance of infolinking in the 21st century cannot be overstated. It is an essential survival skill for students who will continually face more and more new facts, opinions and perspectives from all over the globe.

Librarians as information specialists state unequivocally: *The continuing expansion of information across disciplines demands that all students acquire the thinking skills that will enable them to think on their own. Students must learn to follow an inquiry-based process in seeking knowledge across curricular areas and link ideas in problem solving to make global connections* (American Association of School Librarians, 2008).

The importance of infolinking in the 21st century cannot be overstated. It is an essential survival skill for students who will continually face more and more new facts, opinions and perspectives from all over the globe. The challenge is for the classroom teacher to cover the core content areas and at the same time teach the process of questioning and problem solving. The teacher begins this process by first modeling higher level questions in his or her subject presentations. The next step is for the teacher to instruct the students in the inquiry process so they can learn how to formulate their own questions. Learning to ask questions leads to the reasoning, communicating and applying necessary for problem solving.

The question is *How does the Best Practice teacher get students to deeply understand and connect important content facts and concepts?* Students remember the things they experience. They remember the things that have meaning and have practical applications to their lives. They recall that which has intrinsic value. The teacher facilitates students' recall, understanding and acquisition of knowledge by designing authentic experiences that focus upon:

- Questioning and Observing

- Reasoning and Problem Solving

- Communicating and Applying

The process of questioning and problem solving can best be facilitated by the teacher when he or she understands and can easily incorporate inference questions that ask students to analyze, synthesize and evaluate information in a subject discipline. After questioning is applied in one subject discipline, the next challenge is to create a repertoire of powerful questioning strategies that can be used not only with math, language arts, or science, but across disciplines.

Think About Discussion Questions

1. Rank the four important skills for the 21st century proposed by the American Association of School Librarians. Explain the rationale for your ranking.

2. Bereiter and Scardamalia (2005) suggest that the purpose of the teacher's encouraging dialogic questioning and the process of problem solving is to give students opportunities to generate new knowledge and understandings. Explain how you could encourage dialogic questioning in the subject area or areas you teach.

Reflect on Infolinking and 21st Century Learning

1. Reflect on interdisciplinary learning. Analyze the advantages of using this approach based on what you read in this chapter.

2. Reflect on your own school experience. How much of your learning was interdisciplinary?

Chapter 2

The Socratic Classroom: The Teacher Asks the Questions

Could it be to Socrates that asking questions is teaching?

I am just beginning to see what is behind all your questions. You lead me on by means of things I know, point to things that resemble them, and persuade me that I know things that I thought I had no knowledge of.

- What kinds of questioning skills are important in the 21st century classroom?

- Is questioning synonymous with teaching?

- How does questioning motivate students to learn?

- What is the best way to get students to think about what they are learning?

In the 21st century classroom, time spent focused on the development of analytical questioning and thinking skills is crucial. The activities and behaviors that accompany the presentation of content knowledge either facilitate or limit students' ability to communicate new understandings and link them to the global networked environment which extends beyond the four classroom walls. The goal of the teacher is to strategically facilitate the learning of core knowledge using inquiry-based strategies.

Questioning as Teaching

Great teachers from the past, such as Socrates and Buddha, relied heavily on questions to bring enlightenment to their followers. The Western heuristic method is based on the Socratic method of "teachers ask and students answer." A distinctive feature of this method is that teachers are the decisive factor in the process of teaching and learning. They raise the questions in the beginning and decide on the right answers at the end.

On the contrary, the oriental style of heuristic teaching is based on the principle that students put forward their puzzles and then ask teachers for advice (Zhang, 2007). In this case students ask the questions and try to figure out the answers on their own. They involve the teacher only when they need guidance on how to formulate the next question in a series of problem solving steps.

Questioning has been the topic of educational research for decades. Even if questioning is not always defined as being synonymous with teaching, it has been referred to as a critical part of engaging students in the learning process.

Questioning is a critical part of engaging students in the learning process.

Paulo Freire (1970) believed that questioning was indeed part of the dialogic process. Freire saw the process of opening up dialogue as critical to thinking and the basis of true education. Taba and Inlow stated that *teacher questioning makes the learner more capable of discovering new experiences and more willing to learn for the sake of learning* (Taba and Inlow, 2004). Divergent questions have been noted to be most likely to elicit creative and high level thinking in students' responses (Wilen et al., 2004). They also help students develop the critical and creative thinking skills that are necessary to sort through the rising demands of literacy. Carefully formulated teacher questions can lead to students' developing both critical and creative thinking.

Studies have further referred to "the art of asking questions." This art requires more than the teacher asking questions to receive parroted responses. Display questions to which the teacher knows the answer are not considered as creative. Rather, it is the design of open-ended higher level questions that is referred to as a Best Practice.

Levels of Questioning

One of the most effective strategies a teacher can use is questioning. Teacher directed inquiry draws students into thoughtful interactions and reveals their level of thinking and conceptual understanding. The process of question asking fosters similar inquiry skills in students.

There are two levels of questions: lower level and higher level. Lower level questions require students to recall information that has been registered in memory. These questions ask students to respond using their knowledge base. They are required to perform *one* of the following tasks:

1. to give a definition of a term;

2. to label something using a word or phrase;

3. to supply a specific example;

Studies have further referred to "the art of asking questions." This art requires more than the teacher asking questions to receive parroted responses. Display questions to which the teacher knows the answer are not considered as creative. Rather, it is the design of open-ended higher level questions that is referred to as a Best Practice.

4. to list steps, rules or procedures;

5. to restate conclusions;

6. to provide a predictable answer to a question.

These types of responses focus on specific acceptable answers. Lower level questions are used by the teacher if she or he wants students to focus on the details of a chapter, the math facts or the steps of a laboratory experiment. In the beginning stages of learning, these questions can be valuable. They are also useful for English learners who are at the beginning stages of language development. However, lower level, or rote, responses do little to extend students' thinking.

Higher level questions, on the other hand, stretch students' thinking powers. Higher level questions are concept based and open-ended. These questions demand that students comprehend, apply, analyze, synthesize and evaluate information. They encourage a range of responses and tend to stimulate divergent thinking.

Higher level inquiry questions focus on previously learned knowledge. The teacher poses questions that encourage students to engage in one of the following tasks:

1. to perform an abstract operation;

2. to rate some entity as to its value, dependability or importance and defend the rating;

3. to find similarities or differences in the qualities of two or more entities utilizing a student defined criteria;

4. to make a prediction that is the result of some stated condition, operation or state;

5. to make inferences to account for the occurrence of something (how or why something occurred);

6. to create something new as a result of integrating two or more elements or a number of facts and concepts (Zhang, 2007).

Use lower level questions to focus on details, math facts and procedures. These types of questions focus on recalling information per se.

Use higher level questions to go beyond rote knowledge. Students apply what they've learned to create new possibilities and to solve problems.

Higher level questions can be divided into two types: description and comparison. Description questions require students to observe or describe something using illustrations, demonstrations, maps, graphs or tables. Comparison questions ask students to use statements or illustrations when comparing two things or ideas (Center for Advancement on Learning, 2006).

The teacher can use higher level descriptive questions to encourage students to analyze and synthesize the facts and concepts they are learning. Comparative questions facilitate students' evaluation of information. Both descriptive and comparative questions develop critical and creative thinking skills. Furthermore, questioning strategies engage students in learning and motivate them to pursue additional knowledge on their own.

The following chart illustrates lower and higher levels of questioning.

Levels of Questioning	
Lower	Higher
Requires recall (no processing of data involved)	Requires processing of information
Operates on the level of knowledge • Often superficial • Sometimes trivial	Operates on the higher level of learning including: comprehension, application, synthesis and evaluation. Characteristics: • Potential for depth and acquisition of new insights—results in divergent forms of data processing • Descriptive • Requires observation/description of an object

(Based on Learning Strategies Database: Questioning, Center for Advancement of Learning, Muskingum College, 2008)

Lower and Higher Level Questions

The kinds of questions the teacher verbally asks during instruction influence the level and type of thinking operations in which students are engaged. If the teacher wants students to apply their learning and think like mathematicians, scientists, linguists and social scientists, they must sharpen their questioning skills. Students will usually rise to the thinking level that the teacher poses in his or her questions. Think about the difference between lower and higher level questions in the following disciplines:

An example of a lower level question in language arts is the following: *What is the name of the main character in the story?* This question calls for one correct answer. On the other hand, we can expand on the lower level question, making it into an inference question that requires students to analyze and to evaluate when the teacher asks: *How did the main character's decisions influence the story's outcome?*

Social studies questions can be framed also as lower level or higher level questions. Lower level questions would include the following: *Who was the President of the U.S. during the Civil War? In which state did the Battle of Gettysburg take place?* Just like the language arts example, this social studies knowledge question has one correct answer. It becomes a higher level evaluative question when asked: *How did President Lincoln's actions influence the outcome of the Civil War? Why was the Emancipation Proclamation ordered in 1863 and not in 1861 at the beginning of the War?*

Lower level science questions ask for particular details or definitions: *What are the phases of the moon? Draw them.* This question asks students to recall specific information. Higher level questions on the same topic move students beyond recall to analysis: *The day after a full moon you and some friends are looking at the moon while camping. Your friends want you to explain the Moon's phase at that moment. Explain how the Earth's position in relation to the Moon and the Sun affect the phase of the Moon that you see.*

The kinds of questions the teacher verbally asks during instruction influence the level and type of thinking operations in which students are engaged.

Jerome Bruner did research on how young learners naturally used lower and higher level questioning strategies as they explored their world. Learners relied on their memory to answer simple questions. They were constantly assigning pieces of information to their memory. Learners also used higher level questions and more complex thinking processes. They often posed questions and then used experiments to answer their questions such as the following:

How do flies walk?

Do they have spider webs on their wings?

Do flies grow hair?

How do flies stick to walls upside down?

Do flies know when they are in trouble? (Hervey, 2006)

Young learners' questions approach learning about something from multiple perspectives. The Best Practice teacher uses the same varied questioning that students naturally use. The teacher asks questions that direct students

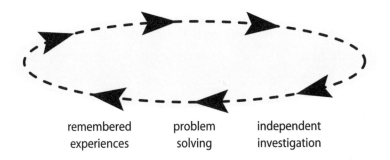

remembered experiences   problem solving   independent investigation

toward the facts and pieces of information that are critical for the foundation of their memory bank. At the same time, the teacher poses questions that lead students to investigate. Students discover how pieces of facts or information can be put together like pieces of a puzzle to solve problems.

In the book, *Banking on Problem Solving in Mathematics*, Robert Wirtz synthesizes Bruner's hierarchy of lower and higher level thinking skills into a continuum.

Wirtz's diagram shows that the lowest level of questioning asks for recall of facts or remembered experiences.

The higher levels of questioning engage students in problem solving. Wirtz states that both lower and higher level questioning may come from others (external) or from oneself (internal). Recall and problem solving questions are usually asked externally by the teacher.

At the highest level of thinking, independent investigation, questions are asked by the students themselves. Usually the questions are prefaced by remarks such as, *Yes, but what if...?* The motivation is intrinsic and often infective. Students who pose their own questions pursue the questions with interest and excitement. Their enthusiasm often draws other students into the search for answers.

The research on Best Practices for teaching mathematics supports the practice of students asking their own questions in the problem solving process. Studies have shown that students who are engaged enough to ask their own questions show higher achievement in mathematics (Salmon-River Eisenhower Project, 2003). Despite this research, studies on teaching practices reveal that 99.9% of the questions asked in the majority of classrooms are posed by the teacher. Another finding was that teachers and many core textbooks used lower level questions, principally focusing on definitions, facts or descriptions (Koufetta et al., 2000). The questions encouraged students to memorize facts rather than to develop deep conceptual understandings. Finally, researchers noted that asking more questions does not guarantee higher level learning and that it is the type, not simply the quantity, of questions that matter (Koufetta et al., 2000).

At the highest level of thinking questions are asked by the students themselves.

The next obvious question is, what kinds of questions engage students in learning and require higher level thinking? Benjamin Bloom, like Wirtz and Bruner, described a hierarchy of thinking skills but in greater detail and with additional levels. Bloom categorized the levels of thinking and showed how these levels could be applied to the teaching and learning process.

Bloom's research revealed that teachers engaged students in higher levels of thinking by asking questions that called for application, analysis, evaluation and synthesis.

The levels of thinking and their applications to learning described in Bloom's research include the following:

- Knowledge: Recalling information learned in the past.

- Comprehension: Understanding the meaning of the recalled information.

- Application: Using acquired understandings in a novel situation.

- Analysis: Disassembling specific information into its components and examining their characteristics and relationships.

- Synthesis: Forming or creating something unique from prior components.

- Evaluation: Assessing information in relation to a set of standards or criteria.

Bloom's hierarchy of thinking skills shows that lower level questions are those at the knowledge, comprehension and simple application levels of the taxonomy. Higher level questions are those requiring complex application, analysis, synthesis and evaluation.

After designing a hierarchy of thinking skills, Bloom extended research on how teachers used these levels of thinking in their daily questioning of students across content areas. Bloom found that the greatest frequency of questions teachers asked required the lowest level of thinking (recall). Bloom's research revealed at the same time that student achievement was correlated to the types of questions teachers asked. Teachers who posed lower level questions had students whose achievement was low. Achievement was, in fact, lower than classrooms where teachers consistently asked students higher level questions.

Bloom's research revealed that student achievement was correlated to the types of questions teachers asked. Teachers who posed lower level questions had students whose achievement was low. Achievement was, in fact, lower than classrooms where teachers consistently asked students higher level questions

	Lower-level		Higher-level	
Bruner:	remembered experiences		problem solving	independent investigation
Bloom:	knowledge comprehension	application	analysis synthesis evaluation	
	Lower-level		Higher-level	

Research has shown that the teacher needs to achieve an appropriate balance between lower and higher level questions. The Best Practice teacher designs questions to elicit specific behaviors. If the teacher wants students to identify the capitals of the states in the United States, he or she asks knowledge or lower level questions. If the teacher wants students to evaluate concepts, he or she must preplan higher level questions.

A Comparison of Hierarchies of Thinking and Levels of Questions

Preplanning questions that are appropriate for each content area helps students achieve at optimum levels. The key word is *preplan*. Oftentimes, teachers who have busy schedules do not take the time needed to plan the higher level thinking questions that deeply probe lesson content. Preplanning includes carefully studying the different types of higher level thinking questions and matching them to content standards and unit topics. Spontaneously creating good questions during classroom instruction is much more difficult than drawing from questions that already have been thought out.

One way to preplan is to think about and formulate questions using the verbs *analyze, evaluate* and *synthesize*. Higher level questions on Bloom's taxonomy emphasize verbs. The verbs used in questions relate to the level of thinking required by students. For example, the verb *identify* is used in the knowledge section. In order to *identify* an even number, the student would have to remember the definition of an even number. Remembering or recalling a definition is a lower level skill on Bloom's hierarchy. A higher level skill *analysis* in mathematics would use the verb *analyze, differentiate, discern* or *discriminate*. In order to differentiate between quadrilaterals and other two-dimension figures, students need to know the specific characteristics of quadrilaterals. They need to find one figure that does not fit the criteria. By using different levels of verbs on Bloom's Taxonomy, students' minds are expanded from remembering facts to applying these facts to solve problems. The *Response Verb Charts* on the following pages give examples of how questions can be expanded from lower to higher levels.

Response Verbs for Levels of Bloom's Taxonomy		
Middle School and High School Science		
Taxonomy Level	**Sample Student Behaviors Response to Questions**	**Example Questions**
Knowledge	identify, name, label, recall, select, define	Which organs in the human alimentary canal produce enzymes that digest proteins?
Comprehension	explain, summarize, compare, contrast, classify, estimate, interpret	What does this graph tell you about how temperature affects the activity of enzymes?
Application	apply, solve, simulate, illustrate, modify, construct, experiment, relate, use, demonstrate	Why does the liver store glucose?
Analysis	discriminate, analyze, dissect, categorize, infer, reason, examine, diagram	What are the pros and cons of storing celery in the refrigerator compared to preserving it with vinegar?
Synthesis	formulate, create, synthesize, generalize, contrive, design, combine, compose, rearrange, invent	How would you create a menu for a diabetic to meet his or her daily nutritional needs?
Evaluation	prioritize, critique, rate, test, measure, assess, grade, rate, rank, evaluate	Which of these meal plans A or B would you recommend for someone with high cholesterol? Explain the reasons for your choice.

(Chin, 2004)

Response Verbs for Levels of Bloom's Taxonomy
Chart One

Taxonomy Level	Sample Student Behaviors in Mathematics Response to Questions				Example Questions
Knowledge Recalling information learned in the past.	count draw recall recite	identify match define list	name label select quote	recognize	*Which number below is an even number?* 3, 117, 208, 19 (identify)
Comprehension Understanding the meaning of the recalled information.	paraphrase explain summarize compare	contrast describe classify estimate	interpret extend		*Which are the next two numbers in the pattern?* 1, 2, 4, 8, ___, ___ (extend)
Application Using acquired understandings in a novel situation.	apply solve simulate illustrate	modify construct experiment relate	use demonstrate		*If Bob is twice as old as his brother Fred, and Fred is 1/5 the age of their 40 year old father, how old is Bob?* (relate, solve)
Analysis Disassembling specific information into its components and examining its characteristics and relationships.	discriminate categorize dissect separate	analyze infer reason detect	diagram order examine		*Which of these figures is not a quadrilateral?* (discriminate)
Synthesis Forming or creating something unique from prior components.	formulate generalize integrate contrive	create design combine develop	predict abstract compose arrange	invent	*Find a rule that describes the number pattern: 0, 1, 3, 7, 15, 31. How could you modify the rule so that all the numbers in the pattern would be even?* (formulate, invent)
Evaluation Assessing information in relation to a set of standards or criteria.	prioritize critique evaluate appraise	measure judge assess grade	rate test rank		*What is the common error in these problems?* 17 42 55 +23 +39 +19 310 711 614 ___ (evaluate)

Classroom Question Classification

Chart Two

Category Name	Expected Cognitive Activity	Key Concepts	Expected Phrases and Questions
Remembering (Knowledge)	Student recalls or recognizes information, ideas, and principles.	memory knowledge repetition description	1. What did the book say about . . . ? 2. Define . . . . 3. List the three . . . . 4. Who invented . . . ?
Understanding (Comprehension)	Student translates, comprehends, or interprets information based on prior learning.	explanation comparison illustration	1. Explain the . . . . 2. What can you conclude . . . ? 3. State in your own words . . . . 4. What does the picture mean? 5. If it rains, then what? 6. What reasons or evidence . . . ?
Solving (Application)	Student selects, transfers, and uses data and principles to complete a problem or task with a minimum of direction.	solution application convergence	1. If you know A and B, how could you determine C? 2. What other possible reasons . . . ? 3. How can you put your data in graphic form? 4. What would happen, do you suppose, if . . . ?
Analyzing (Analysis)	Student distinguishes, classifies, and relates the assumptions, hypothesis, evidence, conclusions, and structure of a statement or a question with an awareness of the thought processes he or she is using.	logic, induction and deduction formal reasoning	1. What was the author's purpose, bias, or prejudice? 2. What must you know for that to be true? 3. Which are facts and which are opinions? 4. What formulas have you learned that support your conclusions?

Classroom Question Classification

Chart Two

Category Name	Expected Cognitive Activity	Key Concepts	Expected Phrases and Questions
Creating (Synthesis)	Student originates, integrates, and combines ideas into a product, plan or proposal that is new to him or her.	divergence productive thinking novelty	1. If no one else knew, how could you find out? 2. Can you describe it in a new way? 3. Make up . . . . 4. What would you do if . . . ?
Judging (Evaluation)	Student appraises, assesses, or criticizes on a basis of specific standards and criteria (this does not include opinion unless standards are made explicit).	judgement selection	1. Which policy will result in the greatest good for the greatest number? 2. For what reason would you favor . . . ? 3. Which of the books would you consider of greater value? 4. Evaluate that idea in terms of cost and community acceptance.

(Ventriglia, 2006)

Open and Closed Questions

Blosser (1995) referred to the use of *closed* and *open* questions. *Closed questions* have a limited number of acceptable responses, most of which will be anticipated by the teacher. They can be further divided into cognitive memory or convergent types.

Cognitive memory questions focus on direct recall of one specific answer. An example of a cognitive memory question is: What is the name of the first President of the United States? Convergent questions, on the other hand, have a varied number of acceptable responses. An example of a convergent question is: What is a synonym for the word edifice? Convergent questions can also extend to higher levels of thinking by asking students to do the following:

- Compare and contrast

  Example: *Based on your observations in today's laboratory activity, what are the differences between healthy and diseased cells?*

- Apply previously learned knowledge

  Example: *Why is it recommended that we use low temperatures when washing gravy stains off synthetic fabrics?*

- Make a judgment

  Example: *If you are a scuba diver submerged 90 feet below the ocean's surface and have only one minute of oxygen left, would you ascend at a rate of 90 feet a minute or would you ascend more slowly, holding your breath for 3 minutes (Chin, 2004).*

Open questions have many acceptable answers, many of which will not be anticipated by the teacher. They promote critical and creative thinking. They encourage students to form hypotheses, speculate about possibilities and invent new solutions. Discussion and analysis is promoted. Students are required to justify their thinking and make judgments based on their background knowledge.

Divergent thinking and evaluative questions are categorized as *Open* questions. One example of a divergent question is: *What would happen if all the land in the world became covered by water?*

An example of an evaluative question is: *What is the best way to report the data on the changing world populations? Is it best to report the data in words, on a chart, on a line graph, on a bar chart or on a pictograph?*

Closed and open questions each have effective applications and can be used across a range of thinking skills. While closed questions focus students' attention on specific details that check understanding, open questions encourage students to generate ideas as well as to promote critical thinking and discussion.

Questioning and Observing

A Best Practice is to encourage active discussions in the classroom (Abbey, 2008). The teacher can promote active dialogue by the type of questions he or she asks. Questions and students' responses can be thought of as an instructional chain of dialogue. The teacher puts the first link in the chain by asking a question. The second link is the student's response. If the teacher asks a closed question, the student responds with a word or phrase and the dialogue stops. There are only two links in the instructional chain.

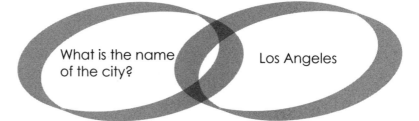

Open ended questions, on the other hand, encourage more discussion. There is no one right answer so the learning dialogue continues as students connect ideas and conclusions.

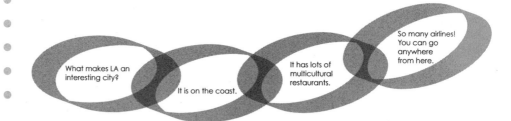

Studies conducted in large numbers of classrooms from elementary school to high school found a significant correlation between academic achievement and a high percentage, at least 70%, of instructional chains that continue dialogue in the classroom (Abbey, 2008). Child-initiated questions lead to dialogic learning as students build on their own knowledge and ideas and chain them into coherent lines of thinking and inquiry (Abbey, 2008).

Inquiry was addressed by Elstgeest (1985) in his guide to productive questions for teachers. The guide included attention focusing, measuring, comparison, action problem-posing and reasoning questions. Productive questioning was thought to stimulate mental activity and reasoning. On the other hand, unproductive questions require bookish, wordy answers that do not encourage thinking.

The teacher uses attention getting questions to guide students in their initial exploration of new materials and to direct their attention to details that they may have overlooked. An example of an attention getting question is: *What was the overriding issue that led to the Civil War? Was it slavery or was it to keep the Union intact?*

The teacher uses measuring questions to get students to move from qualitative to quantitative thinking. Oftentimes, in history and in language arts, the questions are focused only on qualitative evaluations. Measuring questions move students to think about an interdisciplinary perspective. These questions may include: *What were the monetary costs of the Civil War for the North and the South? How could this money have been better used at that time period?*

Comparison questions encourage sharper observation and help students bring order out of chaos (Elstgeest, 1985). A comparison question in science that may be asked is *What do you notice about the differences in structure between bee pollinated flowers and wind pollinated flowers?*

Action questions ask *What happens if…?* For instance, *What happens if I change these numbers to 4, 2 and 1? What happens if I reverse the order of these steps in the experiment? What happens if the United States decides not to trade with Asian countries?*

Problem posing questions serve to challenge students to hypothesize, predict and apply their knowledge in new and creative ways. Elstgeest believed these questions should always start with *Why? Why do students have to spend 12 years in school? Why do you think that a single cell could be a metaphor for a whole community?*

As an inductive process, problem posing questions structure dialogue in the classroom. Along with Elstgeest, many other educators including Dewey, Piaget and Freire advocate this type of inquiry (Shor, 1992). Creating problem posing questions to be used with dialogue is a process that starts with focusing on students' issues that are of deep importance to them.

The teacher begins the problem solving process by asking a series of inductive questions that stimulate students' thinking. The teacher's questions start at the concrete level and move to the analytical level. Students are drawn into the problem solving process as the teacher asks them to name or describe the problem, determine the challenges created by the problem and to generalize the challenges to their own experiences.

As the teacher uses questions to lead students through the process of thinking critically and creatively to solve a problem, he or she expands upon students' responses and background knowledge. It is by connecting new knowledge to existing knowledge that students gain a deeper understanding of subject concepts (Shor, 1992).

Think about teaching the history concept of unequal conditions in society that have existed for minorities and women. This concept can be best taught by relating it to students' understanding of how they felt when they were not permitted to so something that others could do. In this way students come to understand the concept of inequality at a deeper and more personal level.

Wallerstein (1983) refers to the process of creating personal meaning in problem solving as coding. Problem solving and coding are thought to be intertwined. Coding is vital to problem solving because it makes problems relevant to students' lives. Wallerstein suggests that the teacher make interdisciplinary content relevant to students' interests and concerns.

The theme of a literature selection becomes more relevant when students discuss and create written and oral dialogues based on their experiences. History concepts become meaningful as students choose text from a newspaper that relates to a unit of study. Students can also be encouraged to select pictures, slides, photographs, drawings or cartoons to illustrate history concepts. The teacher asks probing critical and creative questions related to students' selections of visuals such as: *How does the picture you have chosen relate to the concept we are studying? What dialogue could you write to explain the meaning of this cartoon? How does this newspaper article capture the theme in our health unit?* These questions are open-ended. They target students' interests and inspire students to reach beyond the concrete to the abstract in learning.

Modeling a Way of Thinking

The teacher's use of effective questioning results in gains in students' achievement. Students who can analyze and reason do better on problem solving and comprehension questions on standardized tests. The instructional emphasis for all levels of questions should be on students gaining a thorough understanding of the subject matter through the use of logical reasoning.

A teacher who asks *why* frequently enough creates students who anticipate the question and ask it of themselves. For example, students who are encouraged to ask *why* while learning mathematical concepts begin to construct compelling mathematical arguments. Students learn to analyze mathematical proofs that have a significant sequence of implications. Students evaluate and explore why one statement follows another (Intersegmental Committee of Academic Senates, 2007).

Best Practice teachers as the instructional leaders in their classrooms ask: *What questions can I use to push my students further in mathematical, scientific, linguistic or historical thinking?* Every subject area is learned more thoroughly when students are encouraged to use critical and creative thinking through the teacher's questioning.

The subject area of science uses the inquiry method to teach important scientific principles. Alke's questioning model is an easy way to help students identify, control and manipulate variables in science experiments.

This method systematically directs the teacher and students to investigate science phenomena through the use of operational questions which manipulate variables through the following:

1. elimination

2. substitution

3. increasing or decreasing the presence of the variables (Chin, 2004).

Teachers can proffer questions during an experiment such as: *What would happen if the few drops of ____ were eliminated in the experiment? What if we substituted ___ for ____? What if we increased __?*

A fifth grade science standard is: *Energy from the sun heats the Earth unevenly, causing air movements that result in changing weather patterns.* The teacher can lead students in their active investigations involving this standard by questions such as: *How does solar energy affect natural processes within the atmosphere, the hydrosphere, and the Earth's surface? How and why do changes in air pressure affect humans and the weather? How do we forecast the weather as it is constantly changing?*

The teacher can stimulate students' to use higher levels of thinking including analysis, evaluation and synthesis before a science experiment at any grade level by asking questions such as: *What are you going to investigate? What is the hypothesis you will be testing? What measurements will you use? How will you record your data? What do you predict will happen?* (Koufetta, 2004)

Research focused on language arts found that the teacher's questions are a form of rehearsal that help students organize information. Dickenson (1990) as well as Osman and Hoffman (1994) found that the use of questions improves the performance of students in mastering English language arts standards. Effective questions do not just have students retrieve information from the text, rather they involve students in the literature they are reading.

Questions that stimulate the discussion of a literature selection focus on having students relate to the characters' experiences and challenges. The teacher's questions lead students to create innovative solutions to the challenges that the characters faced. Students are encouraged to use evidence from the text to support their ideas. The following are examples of questions that lead to students actively sharing ideas: *How did the character's personality contribute to his fate at the end of the story? Can you describe a situation in the story where the character's actions led to his demise?*

One questioning technique that can be used successfully with literature at any grade level is entitled *Questioning the Author* (Beck, 2000). In the traditional approach to comprehension, students wait until they are finished reading to deal with the text's ideas. *Questioning the Author* teaches students "to grapple with ideas as they initially encounter them in text" (Beck and McKeown, 2002).

This method has the teacher prompt students to put ideas together. The teacher uses two kinds of probes, *Initiating Queries* and *Follow-up Queries*. The Teacher uses initiating queries such as *What is the author trying to say? What do you think the author means by that?* Follow-up queries include: *How does this information connect to what the author said earlier? Why did the author describe the way the character acted in detail?*

These questions are meant to stimulate conversations. Beck and McKeown state that discussion increases student engagement and comprehension. Spiral questioning throughout the reading of a literature selection was also noted to be more effective than questions asked at the end of a selection.

This technique works well with struggling readers and English learners because the teacher can read or preview the story or expository passage with students. She or he can then involve students in a discussion using targeted questions before they read the story or passage themselves. This alerts students to the important ideas. In a study of 6th grade struggling readers, researchers found discussion using "Initiating Queries and Follow-Up Queries" facilitated students' comprehension by providing them opportunities to reflect on ideas (Sandora et al., 1999).

Using the strategy of *Questioning the Author* also helps students make sense out of social science texts. This happens as students learn to view texts as "just someone else's ideas written down" (Beck and McKeown, 2002).

Consider the 5th grade social studies standard *Students explain the causes of the American Revolution* (California Standards for Social Sciences, 1998). Instead of having students answer questions on the causes of the American Revolution at the end of a chapter, the teacher would guide students through his or her use of questioning in critically thinking about a chapter. The teacher does this by first formulating an overall question such as: *What do students need to take away from the text in order to understand the major causes of the American Revolution?* Once this is determined, then small chunks of text are analyzed through the use of questioning. The following example is based on Beck and McKeown.

Social Studies Textbook Selection (Based on excerpt)	Questions for the Author
Events Leading to the Revolutionary War Rebellion in Virginia William Berkeley, the king's chosen governor, kept a firm grip on the government of Virginia. He handpicked his advisors...He personally choose the people to run the courts (Beck and McKeown, 2002).	The teacher would stop after this paragraph and ask the following questions: What is the author telling us about Governor Berkeley? What does the author mean by saying that he was "the king's chosen governor? Why does the King and not the colonists get to choose the Governor for the American colonies? How do you think the colonists felt about having a Governor that they did not choose? How does this fit into what we learned about the colonists? (Beck and McKeown, 2002).

The *Questioning the Author* technique has value in helping students gain deep knowledge in content areas. In social studies, for example, students who are reading often become distracted by facts and fail to grasp the real conceptual understandings. The teacher's effective use of this technique not only helps students comprehend the social studies text but also teaches them to view reading as an active process of constructing meaning rather than extracting information (Beck and McKeown, 2002).

Constructing meaning in a new language is one of the primary tasks of English learners. The teacher can help these students by *scaffolding* questions to the language proficiency level of English learners. Students need to be able to comprehend and respond to what is being asked. The teacher can help beginning language learners by rephrasing the vocabulary and simplifying the question type and sentence structure. Beginning students can be asked questions such as: *What is this?, Where is the _____?, What is_____?, Is this a ____ or a _____?* Then these questions can be expanded to *Why* and *What do you think* questions. The thing to remember is that English learners can think critically and creatively. When they start to learn the language, they may not have the words to express themselves. The importance of questions for English learners is that the questions help stimulate discussion.

For all students, the teacher's "art of asking questions" stimulates discussions and conceptual understanding across subject areas. Best Practice teachers as instructional leaders in their classrooms ask *What questions can I use to push my students further in critical and creative thinking?*

It is important that the teacher consider the following as they implement both lower level and higher level questioning matched to basic foundational skills and conceptual understandings:

- Talk less and ask more.

- Use more divergent questions.

- Reduce the number of questions that can be answered by *yes* or *no*.

- Develop questioning throughout content learning both from texts and through hands-on experiments and activities..

- Create an atmosphere of trust so students feel encouraged to ask their own questions.

- Respond in an encouraging way.

- Include student questions throughout the lesson..

- Use questions that stimulate deeper thinking.

- Reflect upon the levels of thinking elicited by different types of questions.

- Identify the cognitive skills and conceptual processes you want your students to engage in and then construct questions to elicit the desired thinking.

- Pay attention to the wording of questions to extend thinking.

- Look for questioning opportunities in each and every lesson.

- Increase the wait time to at least five seconds.

- Have students use higher level question stems.

- Have students question a partner.

- Have students write responses to questions.

Wait time is particularly important in the "art of questioning." After asking a question, teachers often want an immediate answer. Research is clear in noting that wait time must be at least 5 seconds to get the best students' responses (Chin, 2004). Studies found that when teachers extended their wait time to 3 seconds or more, the length of students' responses, the incidence of critical and creative thinking, students' understanding and achievement all increased (Rowe, 1987). Furthermore, Tobin found that teachers who increased their wait time asked fewer lower level questions and more probing and application questions.

Constructing New Understandings

Good questions lead students to think and utilize the knowledge that they already have to construct new understandings. Questioning strategies also encourage students to learn from one another. The Project IMPACT Study showed the importance of questioning strategies to learning. At risk students and advanced students were used in a study that measured the effects of questioning strategies. The results of the study found that effective questioning resulted in academic gains for all students. The teacher's use of good questioning enabled learners to analyze and solve problems for themselves in ways that made sense to them (Rowan and Robles, 2007). The following are questions that can be used in different content areas and across content areas to encourage active learning and high academic achievement.

Questions and Prompts for Making Sense of Mathematics

These are questions and prompts that the teacher can use to help students make sense out of mathematics:

- Did anyone get the same answer in a different way?

- Did anyone get a different answer? How did you arrive at your answer?

- What did you analyze or evaluate to discover the answer?

- Tell the class what you were thinking.

- Can you explain how you got your answer to a partner?

- What is another way to get the same answer?

Questions that Foster Reasoning in Mathematics and Science

These questions foster reasoning and critical thinking processes:

- Will what you did always work out that way? How do you know?

- Do you see a pattern in this? What is it? What would make it easier to see?

- How could the problem be completed in a shorter way?

- What other numbers or facts can be arranged to reach the same conclusion?

- Are there some numbers or facts that will not work in the equation? How do you know?

- Write a new problem that is different in some ways and the same in others.

- What is the largest number you can think of that will work? What is the smallest?

Questions and Prompts for Predicting, Inventing and Problem Solving

These questions foster predicting, inventing and problem solving:

- What would happen if…?

- Is there a pattern? Why or why not?

- What decisions can you make from this pattern?

- What is the same and different about your two ways of doing this? (This question could refer to two ways by the same students or by two different students.)

Questions and Prompts that Foster Self Reliance

These are questions and prompts that encourage students to rely more on themselves:

- Does this make sense to you? Why or why not?

- What would seem more reasonable to you?

- How can you check to see for yourself if the answer is correct?

- What do you think you should do next?

- Please explain your way of solving the problem to the class.

- Make a model (use materials or a drawing) to show how you solved the problem.

- Find a classmate and see if you can solve the problem together.

Questions that Foster Connecting and Applying Mathematics Across Disciplines

These are questions and prompts that help students connect and apply mathematics within and across subject disciplines:

- Have you ever solved a problem like this before?

- How does this relate to ___ (what we learned in___)? (interdisciplinary)

- Tell (or write) a story problem about this concept.

- How does this relate to what we did in science (or another subject) the other day?

- What would you measure it with? Why?

- How do you think a carpenter (or any real-life worker) would use this mathematics concept?

- Can you write [a sentence, paragraph, story] or draw a picture to explain how you figured out the solution to the problem? (interdisciplinary)

- Use these materials to show how you solved the problem. Do you think other materials would work better?

- How many different kinds of mathematics were used in these science investigations? (interdisciplinary)

- What is different about the mathematics used in these two situations?

- Where would this problem fit on our mathematics chart?

(Reprinted with the permission from Teaching Children Mathematics, National Council of Teachers of Mathematics)

Questions that Foster Connecting and Applying Concepts from Social Science and History

These are questions and prompts that help students connect and apply what they are learning in social science. These questions help students use the same critical thinking processes used by a historian.

- How are we connected to events and people of the past?

- Analyze how technology has influenced innovations in science, social science, education and mathematics. (interdisciplinary)

- What is the relationship between work and money?

- Evaluate how past decisions and actions affect future choices. (interdisciplinary)

- How did people at this time view the world? Is this view still applicable today? (interdisciplinary)

- If this happens, how will the political consequences affect society?

- What do we need to do to make things change?

- How does geography affect history, economics, government and the culture of people? (interdisciplinary)

Questions for United States and World History and Global Literacy (Grades 9-12)

- Analyze how global conflict/cooperation shaped the course of U.S. history.

- Evaluate how the United States has viewed its role in the global community. (interdisciplinary)

- Analyze how geography, climate and natural resources influence culture. (interdisciplinary)

- Evaluate how natural resources contribute to the economic wealth of a nation. (interdisciplinary)

- Evaluate how economic markets have influenced the evolution of U.S. history.

- Evaluate how world governments can cooperate to make ethical decisions related to our global environment (Ratway, 2009).

- How has the global economy changed by actions undertaken by governments?

- What are the implications of this political event for the present scientific community? Evaluate the impact of this event on the future. (interdisciplinary)

Questions that Foster Connecting and Applying Concepts from English Language Arts, Literature and Foreign Language

These questions help students think about what they are reading and apply it to their own lives and across disciplines.

English Language Arts and Literature

- What were the biggest challenges facing the main character in the story? How are these similar to challenges you face?

- If you could meet two characters from this story, which ones would you like to meet and why.

- Compare and contrast these two advertisements on _____. (interdisciplinary)

- Rank the ten most important facts you learned in this article. Explain why you ranked the facts in this order. (interdisciplinary)

- How have people used symbols to preserve and represent the values of their cultural groups? (interdisciplinary)

- Evaluate which of these articles gave the most persuasive argument. (interdisciplinary depending on the subject areas of the expository readings)

- After reading the two perspectives on whether cars should or should not be allowed to drive on the beach, which point of view do you agree with? How would you support your choice by citing future consequences using scientific, economic and historic resources? (interdisciplinary reasons)

- Who are the candidates in the mayoral election? Read press releases in the newspaper and online about these candidates. Evaluate which of the candidates has the best chance of implementing the changes he or she has set forth in the future. What evidence, logic or facts can you offer to support your position?

Foreign or Global Language

- Explain the meaning of this idiom in English. What cultural understandings must you have to understand this idiom?

- Analyze what these words in _____ have in common. If you had to teach these words to someone else, what strategies would you teach them to remember the words?

- Evaluate the challenges you would face in trying to invent a new world language.

- Create two new idioms in English or in another language to convey an idea. Create an argument to explain the reasons the idioms that you created are useful.

- If you could instantly learn three global languages, which ones would you choose? Explain the reasons for your choice. Evaluate how learning these languages would improve your life and future career choice. (interdisciplinary)

Questions that Foster Connecting and Applying Concepts from Science, Health and Physical Education

These questions are examples of connecting and applying concepts from the sciences, health and physical education:

- What do you need to know to _____?

- How does understanding a living thing's basic needs help you to create an environment that will help it grow?

- Analyze how fossils provide us with information about animals and cultures from the past? (interdisciplinary)

- How do people and groups of organisms interact with their environments? Evaluate whether these interactions are beneficial or harmful to the environment. (interdisciplinary)

- Analyze how eating habits and exercise affect maintaining a healthy heart.

- Evaluate which has a greater impact on people's health: water or air pollution.

Asking Questions that Promote 21st Century Thinking

The critical thinking skills students need to be successful in the 21st century are problem solving, synthesis and analysis. They need to be able to infolink the information on the ever increasing 500 million information links that currently exist on the World Wide Web. These links will continue to grow as information expands at exponential rates.

These are the types of questions teachers can ask that will enable students to survive and prosper in a continually changing technological environment.

Checking for Understanding

Students understand, define or explain the problem or task.

- Can you tell me how you got that answer?

- What can you tell me about _____?

- Would you please explain that in your own words?

- How would you relate this to _____?

- Which statements support _____?

- What is the main idea of _____?

- Can you write an explanation in your journal?

- Can you write the author's conclusion in your own words?

Using Research Strategies and Technology

Students use research strategies to solve problems. They record information. They use technology and other multimedia sources that foster nonlinear learning.

- How can you formulate a question to get this information on the World Wide Web?

- How can you organize this information on a computer spreadsheet?

- How can you evaluate the importance of the information you found?

- What sources did you find that use reliable statistics?

- Analyze how you can use the following computer link to solve the problem.

- Create a question based on what you read. Use the World Wide Web to answer your question.

Comparing and Contrasting

Students compare and contrast facts related to the problem and solution.

- Compare and contrast _____.

- Do you see a pattern in these facts from these two websites?

- Can you create a Venn diagram to illustrate what is the same and what is different?

- What can you invent that would change the results?

- How can you research the data you need to answer this question using three Internet sites?

- Compare your results to the results of the students in your group.

Estimating and Conjecturing

Students make educated guesses.

- Can you estimate or predict the answer to this question?

- What questions can you ask to help you solve the problem?

- How can you create a graphic organizer to show the relationship among facts?

- Is there a way to use an outline and webbing to formulate questions?

- Is there a way to use the following WebQuests to formulate the most relevant questions for solving the problem?

Using Conversations for Learning

Students use conversations to help articulate their thought processes. They clarify their thinking by talking to their peers.

- Can you explain your thinking to a partner?

- Create a question that would help you solve this problem with a partner.

- Create a graphic organizer with your group to explain your group's thinking or position.

- Create a new solution by infolinking these interdisciplinary facts and concepts with a partner.

Creating Original Hypotheses and Ideas

Students create original hypotheses and ideas.

- Can you think of two new ways to solve the problem?

- How would you improve _____?

- What would happen if _____?

- How would you invent a new way of doing _____?

- What change would you make to solve _____?

Participating in Paired and Cooperative Learning Groups

Students work together to solve problems and invent new solutions.

- Who do you want to work with you to solve this problem?

- How can you explain your idea to your group using a picture or another visual?

- How did your team leader contribute to your group working together successfully?

- How can you help your group understand your thinking by creating a brief outline?

- How would you evaluate your group's solution to the problem?

Documenting Thinking

Students document and support their thinking.

- What steps did you take to find the answer? Could you have eliminated some of the steps?

- How can you make a visual display of your results?

- Can you make a chart or table to explain your results to the class?

- How can you verify that your thinking is correct?

- Can you create a graphic organizer to show the steps n your thinking?

- Can you create a story about your results?

- Can you create an illustration to show your results?

Forming Interdisciplinary Generalizations

Students form interdisciplinary generalizations. Students connect their ideas to other similar problems and to real-life situations.

- What generalizations can you make from this interdisciplinary data?

- How are these issues like the ones you learned in _____?

- Can you think of a rule for solving this kind of problem that would extend across other subject areas?

- How can you apply your thinking to the solution of this school problem, community challenge or global issue?

- What real world applications does this have?

- How can you link the information from several sources to come up with a solution to the problem?

All these questions focus on 21st century critical and creative thinking. The Best Practice teacher ensures that students have a foundation in the facts and skills of each content area. The teacher also extends students' learning through higher level questioning.

The use of 21st century inference questions prepares students to function in the technological, highly information-based global environment. The teacher's modeling of effective questions enables students to ask their own strategic questions, which in essence is the goal of 21st century learning.

Think About Discussion Questions

1. Think about the Questioning the Author Strategy (Beck and McKeown, 2004) on pages 31-32. Write three questions using this strategy for one subject area content standard you teach. If you teach math or science, write three questions instead for one of your units of study using the Alke model on pages 29-30.

2. Rank the categories of 21st century questions on pages 42-45 in what you believe to be their importance for 21st century learning. Give a rationale for your ranking system.

Reflection on Questioning Techniques

1. Reflect on the type of questioning you use in your classroom. Write the type of questions you ask most frequently? Evaluate the questions. Are they higher level or lower level questions?

2. Reflect on your subject textbook for one unit of study. Take at least 5 questions and analyze each one according to Bloom's taxonomy.

Chapter 3

The Heuristic Function of Language: Students Ask the Questions

Which length of stick should I use to turn the square into a cube?

"The important thing is not to stop questioning."

—*Albert Einstein*

The Heuristic Function of Language

One of the most important functions of language is the asking of questions. This is labeled by the famous linguist Michael Halliday as the heuristic function of language. Halliday describes this language function as important for learners to gain knowledge about their environment (Halliday, 1975). Young learners naturally ask questions. They want to know why the sun doesn't fall out of the sky. They want to know how things work. This natural curiosity is usually encouraged by parents and often discouraged once the learner begins his or her formal education. Students become less prone to ask questions as they move through the grade levels (Exline, 2009).

McKenzie states that the secret to effective research with new electronic information is the use of powerful questioning strategies. In fact, questions may be one of the most powerful technologies invented by humans.

A common Western method of classroom instruction is to have the teacher ask the questions. This fact is noted in research studies on classroom communication. Hyman reported that there were 38 teacher questions to every one student question in the typical U.S. classroom (Hyman, 1980). Other researchers who documented classroom interactions found the number of teacher questions at the ratio of 52 questions to every one student question.

The ratio of teacher to student questions is considered very important to the learning process. The formulation of questions by students implies that they have thought about what they are learning. They are able to apply critical and creative thinking to their content knowledge.

The ability to formulate critical and creative questions is a critical skill for the 21st century learner. McKenzie states that *the secret to effective research with new electronic information is the use of powerful questioning strategies. In fact, questions may be one of the most powerful technologies invented by humans.*

The goal of the Best Practice classroom is to have a higher ratio of student questions. While the use of open-ended or higher level questioning encourages students to ask their own questions to apply knowledge, one right answer questioning decreases critical thinking.

The Right Answer System

The Right Answer System can be defined as a method of instruction where there is a single right answer to every question (Schank, 2009). Standardized tests encourage the right answer system. The Right Answer System encourages students to focus on one answer rather than on formulating questions that may lead to expanded learning. This does not mean that students do not need to learn the right answers for addition or multiplication problems. It does not mitigate the need for students to acquire basic facts and principles across subject areas. On the contrary, the content of disciplines is very important, but as a means to an end, not as an end in itself (Exline, 2009). The knowledge base for disciplines is constantly expanding and changing. No one can ever learn all the facts which continue to grow exponentially.

Evolution of Individual and Cumulative Human Knowledge
Learning: A Process for Individuals From Birth to Death
Learning: A Process for Human Society Throughout Its History

UNKNOWN

Known → Known → Known → Known

UNKNOWN

home ←→ school ←→ society

(Exline, 2009)

Schank (2009) states when information enters the memory without a real connection to the world, it is quickly forgotten because there is no meaningful place for the learning to reside.

The exponential growth of knowledge in the 21st century makes it impossible for students to remember millions of isolated facts. Rather, 21st century learning becomes a process of students linking or connecting relevant facts to their knowledge of the world. Schank (2009) states *when information enters the memory without a real connection to the world, it is quickly forgotten because there is no meaningful place for the learning to reside.*

Meaningful connections are made by students through the inquiry process and through self-generated questions. As students formulate questions based on interrelated facts, they begin to link and expand their content knowledge base.

The following chart shows how student generation of questions is tied to content knowledge.

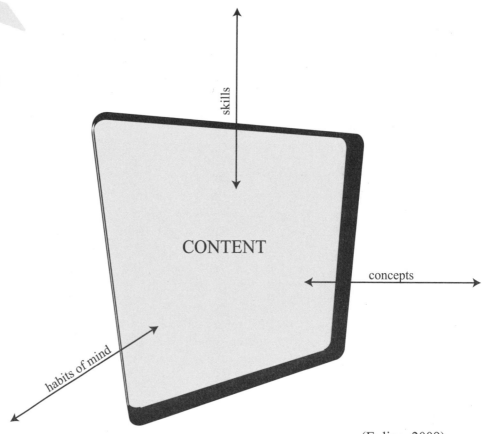

Essentials for Effectively Generating and Transmitting the Fund of Knowledge

skills

CONTENT

concepts

habits of mind

(Exline, 2009)

Generating questions is much more difficult than generating answers. Even factual questions are difficult to formulate for some learners. It is interesting that one of the exercises recommended for English learners is for them to formulate questions from statements. Yet, English only students are not asked to do this important exercise which is the first step to learning how to ask questions. Learning to ask questions through the process of inquiry is important for all students. Most students have not learned how to formulate questions. In order to understand and process information both at lower and higher level thinking levels, students must develop a repertoire of questioning strategies which includes learning to ask the following five types of questions:

1. Knowledge-Based Questions: *Fact or Foundation Questions*

2. Learning to Ask Critical Thinking Questions: *Why Questions*

3. Learning to Ask Research Questions: *Why and Apply Questions*

4. Learning to Ask Creative Right Brain Directed Questions: *Imagine Questions*

5. Learning to Ask Questions Related to Nonlinear Formats: *Strategic Questions*

Learning to Ask Knowledge Based Questions: Fact or Foundation Questions

Learning to ask factual questions lays a foundation for all future learning. Foundation questions give students the basic information they need for a more in-depth study of any subject area. *What questions* build the foundation to acquire facts? An example of a foundation question is *What is the capital of California?*

Knowledge questions are linear. Students move from the question to the answer in a direct line or directly from the question to the answer. The question A) *What is the capital of California?* moves to the direct linear answer B) *The capital of California is Sacramento.* Foundation or factual questions are very important because they provide the structure or scaffolding for all knowledge.

Learning how to formulate factual or knowledge questions is the beginning of the inquiry process. Asking questions is a process of transformation. Information is transformed from statements to questions. The process of transforming knowledge through inquiry takes practice. The process begins by having students take factual statements and turn them into questions.

The facts are used as "chunks of language." The facts are not analyzed; they are taken verbatim. Factual questions are

taught with the questioning words *What, Where, Who, How, How Many* or other similar words. Students are given these words and then are asked to formulate questions choosing one of these words. This process still takes thinking and some students may struggle at first to choose the correct word.

This is an example of how a math statement can be changed to a question.

Statement: *An octagon has eight sides.*

Question: *How many sides does an octagon have?*

A statement relating to history may be changed to a simple question in the same way.

Statement: *The United States has a democratic form of government.*

Question: *What form of government does the United States have?*

After students become proficient in changing statements to questions, they should be encouraged to think of multiple questions that can be asked about a statement. The following is a series of questions related to a statement from a language arts text.

Statement: *The author of this article was born in the 18th century in Paris.*

Questions: *When was the author of the article born?*
Where was the author of the article born?
How many centuries ago was the author born?

Another technique is to teach students to generate knowledge questions in a paired situation. The teacher poses a scenario and then has students ask questions to find information. For example, *this is a map of the city. You need to get to the train station. What questions would you ask to get directions?*

Students can also write questions for a survey. The survey can cross subject areas from language arts to math and science. An example in language arts would be to interview a fellow student or to role play interviewing a famous person. Both students read about the person. Then they both formulate questions using the question stems to ask each other.

Learning to ask factual questions is the first step in developing a repertoire of questioning strategies that students can use in learning.

As students' sophistication with question-asking grows, they can start to apply critical and creative questioning. Even Kindergarten students can begin to categorize questions into *Fact* questions, *Why* Questions and *Imagine* Questions. Students in upper elementary can label questions as *Knowledge Questions, Critical Thinking Questions* and *Creative Thinking Questions*. Middle school and high school students can develop their own categories for different types of questions. They can create a Question Chart with a partner to find information and then analyze and critique any topic. They can also crosslink questions to other disciplines.

Learning to Ask Critical Thinking Questions: Why Questions

Critical thinking questions require students to move from a linear transformation process to a nonlinear transformation process. These questions are nonlinear and open ended. Students are required to integrate discrete pieces of information into new knowledge and fresh insights. Students ask questions that move in a circular rather than a straight path. The circle of questions manifests that questioning really never ends. Rather, posed questions lead to a series of new questions.

Students learn to ask transformative critical thinking questions when they move from stating knowledge to constructing their own understandings of knowledge through examining, discussing, working on challenging problems and dealing with competing points of view (Mavericks, 2009).

Some students naturally ask higher level questions. Others need to be encouraged by the teacher to practice asking open-ended questions that lead to multiple answers. One way to encourage students to practice critical thinking questioning is through the use of analysis and synthesis question stems. The challenge is for students to create open-ended questions that lead to a chain of questions: *What must you know to conclude that _____? How can you analyze the ways that ____? How can you synthesize this information to come up with a new ____? What are other possible reasons? What would happen if you combined _____?*

Question Chart

Knowledge Questions

* What is the name of_____?

* How is the _____put together?

* Where is the_____?

Critical Thinking Questions

* What evaluation can I use to_____?

* Which are the facts and opinions?

* How can I analyze_____?

Creative Thinking Questions

* What if_____?

* What is a new way to connect_____?

* What is a new way to_____?

* What are the new insights I have learned?

Through authentic practice opportunities, students quickly come to understand the difference in questions that have one right answer and questions that have multiple answers.

The 21st century questions listed on pages 42-46 can be listed on a chart in the classroom or given to students as a handout. The point is for students to practice using the different types of questions. Students can practice formulating questions before a topic is presented. For example, the teacher might say the following: *Write two research questions about this topic.*

During a subject presentation students may be asked to generate questions that compare and contrast information such as: How does this relate to _____? At the end of a unit of study, students might be asked to write questions that connect what they learned to other subject disciplines. A science unit on pollution might be related to health with a multidisciplinary question such as: *What if all the cities in the United States were polluted by smog. How would this impact global health?*

The ASK (Analyze, Synthesize, Knowledge) strategy directs students to formulate questions that enable them to analyze and synthesize the information from two or more sources. For example, *How are the ideas in the two sources alike? How can they be connected and integrated to devise a new plan for _____?*

Students can learn to apply critical thinking questions to the core curriculum as well as related subject area disciplines. Students use inquiry first to find out why. The second task is to use inquiry to formulate alternate scenarios on how to apply what they have learned (Murray, 2007).

Learning to Ask Research Questions: Why and Apply Questions

Learning to ask *why* is only part of the research or problem solving process. Students must also learn to formulate questions that enable them to apply what they have learned. Davis (1982) outlines some strategies that she calls *Super Think* strategies that encourage learners to formulate questions that

The ASK (Analyze, Synthesize, Knowledge) strategy directs students to formulate questions that enable them to analyze and synthesize the information from two or more sources.

include both the *why* and *apply* part of critical questioning. Davis states that students usually approach research as a process of finding and copying information on a particular topic. They rarely think of research as a way to generate additional questions and new knowledge. She suggests that research projects begin with students writing a list of *why* and *apply* questions. Questions that integrate the *why* and *apply* can be used very effectively across subject disciplines. These are some examples: *Why did this happen this way? How can I apply this knowledge to change events in the future? What would be another way to ___? How can these alternatives be applied to _____? If I change the date on this information from 1809 to 2009, how would I have to update the information? What would be two other ways to apply ____?* (Doyle, 2009)

Critical questioning is also learned through open-ended investigations and experiments. Students learn to ask questions in a meaningful context. Giving students questions that can be applied at the beginning of an investigation helps them construct their own questions. Any subject area can be used as a topic for an open-ended investigation. These are seven critical questions that can be used by students to think about how to research any topic across subject areas:

1. *What do I know about this topic?*

2. *Are there different ways to gather information on this topic?*

3. *Are there different ways of measuring ____?*

4. *What will happen if _____?*

5. *In what ways can I record my data?*

6. *What applications does the data have?*

7. *Are there any applications that relate to social science, health, etc? (Wetzel. 2008).*

Students develop a better understanding of any concept when they work on authentic problems and explorations that have relevance outside the school walls. As students create their own research questions, the learning becomes more meaningful to them. Questioning for creative research involves the following

Giving students questions that can be applied at the beginning of an investigation helps them construct their own questions.

phases:

- **Planning:** Formulating an open-ended question to be addressed by the research project in language arts, history, science, health or any subject area.

  What if the South had won the Civil War?

  How would our lives be different today?

  How is a verb like a baseball game?

- **Retrieving:** Formulating questions to collect multiple sources of data.

  What sources of information can be added to_____?

  What does this information make me think about?

  What references give general information? What references give specifics?

  What are some keywords that I can use to get more data?

  What are the smallest pieces I can break this data into?

- **Linking:** Formulating questions to link together information.

  How does this relate to _____?

  What can I create by connecting these facts to those?

  What is the best way to organize and integrate this data?

  Do the footnotes and links on the websites add valuable information?

- **Evaluating:** Formulating questions to evaluate the data and the sources that have been used to collect the data.

  What have I learned from the data I collected?

  Which sources of data are most applicable?

  Is the statistical data I collected current enough?

  What type of domain does the data come from?

  What are the author's credentials on the subject?

- **Reflecting:** Formulating questions to reflect on new content knowledge.

   How can I think of multiple ways to integrate what I learned to answer my strategic question?

   What new insights have I gained?

   How can I connect the data in a new way that will lead to a new solution to the problem?

   How can I best communicate what I have learned?

The questions for creative research enable students to utilize knowledge-based facts, analysis and synthesis to answer an open-ended research question. By asking questions at each phase of the research or problem-solving process, students can effectively organize data and generate multiple insights for answers and solutions.

Learning to Ask Creative Right Brain Directed Questions: Imagine Questions

Critical and creative questioning are interrelated and complementary aspects of thinking. While critical questioning requires the skills of analytic thinking, creative questioning focuses on exploring ideas and generating possibilities. Both critical and creative questioning are important in problem solving. Critical questioning helps students formulate questions to analyze a problem. Creative questioning then enables students to generate a number of solutions to the problem. Learning how to ask creative questions enables students to see beyond what they already know or believe to be possible to something innovative or new. The following chart delineates the difference between critical and creative questions.

Critical and creative questioning are interrelated and complementary aspects of thinking. While critical questioning requires the skills of analytic thinking, creative questioning focuses on exploring ideas and generating possibilities.

Critical Thinking Questions: *Why?*	Creative Thinking Questions: *What If?*
Analytic: What must you know for that to be true?	Generative: If this is true, then what are some other possibilities?
Convergent: What formulas have you learned that support your conclusions?	Divergent: How can you use the formulas you have learned to create a ____?
Vertical: If A is true, then B is ___?	Lateral: If A is true, what is something new that would change B?
Probability: What can you conclude from these facts given what you know?	Possibility: What if the facts were changed? What would be some possible new conclusions?
Judgment: What is the author's purpose?	Nonjudgment: If no one else knew this author, how would you advertise this book?
Focused: What is the rule you can apply to this number pattern?	Diffused: How could you modify the rule so that ___?
Objective: Analyze the facts in this case?	Subjective: Can you describe the facts in a new way?
Linear: What step do you do next?	Associative: How can you make up a new way to connect these steps to develop the idea of ____?
Reasoning: Which are facts and opinions?	Novelty: How can you change the facts in the story to create a new ending?

(Harris, 2009)

This chart shows that critical questioning is based on vertical thinking in which students move from one logical step to the next, always moving toward the correct answer (Schrock, 2009). Critical questioning aims to create questions that point to one solution and exclude others. Creative questioning, on the other hand, generates multiple paths to the solution. The idea is for students to use creative questions to attack problems differently without the artificial restraints usually applied to problem solving.

DeBono refers to out-of-the-box creative questioning which has no limitations as lateral thinking. Questioning tied to lateral thinking generates a multitude of possibilities. Students can generate numerous *What if* questions. These questions enable students to synthesize facts and concepts to come up with something new. The teacher helps the student master Right Brain Directed questions by encouraging students to formulate questions that take them from *what is* to *what could be* (DeBono, 1970).

Creative questioning often requires the higher level skill of synthesis. It has often been labeled as part of the right brain intuitive process. Pink calls the 21st century the Conceptual Age where creative questioning is the key to students' success in the global workforce (Pink, 2006). Creative questioning in its simplest form is referred to by Pink as the act of creating solutions through design. Designing something new causes students to formulate questions and "think out of the box." One activity suggested by Pink is to design a new object for something that annoys you.

The students, for example, might design a new type of furniture for their classroom. To design the object, students must first think of a series of questions relating to the new design. These questions can be stated orally to a partner, discussed and then written down. Brainstorming with a partner or in a group setting often facilitates creative questioning. The questions would include *If we changed this to ___, then ___?* (Pink, 2006)

A technique that aids the teacher in helping students to design questions that lead to out-of-the-box thinking is SCAMPER (Eberle, 1997). This technique enables students to change a product or idea into something new or innovative through: *Substitute. Combine, Add, (Modify, Magnify and Minify), Put to Other Uses, Eliminate* and *Reverse*. The SCAMPER process takes a statement and then asks a number of questions. The following statement is an example of how the SCAMPER process can be applied.

A study at Georgetown University found that even if students, teachers and the educational process remained the same, improving a school's physical environment could increase test scores by 11% (www.cabe.org.uk).

> **Creative questioning often requires the higher level skill of synthesis. It has often been labeled as part of the right brain intuitive process.**

S (Substitute) What can be changed about the school's physical environment?

C (Combine) What aspects of the school environment can be combined to create something new?

A (Add) What would the school environment look like if it was created for 21st century learning? What needs to be added?

M (Modify) What could be modified?

P (Put to Other Uses) How can what exists be put to other uses?

E (Eliminate) What would be the effect of changing the school's physical environment?

R (Reverse) What would be the opposite or antithesis of this change?

The SCAMPER method can be used with any subject area to have students implement the creative questioning process. This method calls for creative and inventive thinking to take something from what is to what could be. It is one of the most important types of questioning for the 21st century.

Ensemble Story Teaching is another way to develop creative questioning through drama and the arts. This process can be extended from kindergarten to high school. Stories are recreated through the use of story-based inquiry. As the drama unfolds, so do the questions. For example, instead of reading about the Civil War, students use drama and story to engage in the war as a soldier or a nurse. Students then question the person about their feelings, about their actions and about the time in history. Students can manipulate and change scenarios to learn multiple perspectives on an event in history or in a literature selection. Younger children can use a story like the *Hungry Caterpillar*. Students can become the caterpillar. A series of questions can be generated that relate to the feelings and consequences of the caterpillar's actions. Then students can create a new scenario by having the caterpillar take different actions (Cordi, 2009). Creative questioning allows students to use their imaginations. It is one of the most important types of questioning strategies because it encourages students to put together the myriads of 21st century facts in new and different ways.

Learning to Ask Questions Related to Nonlinear Formats: Strategic Questions

The process of inquiry on the World Wide Web is structured around vocabulary knowledge and strategic questioning. Students are most successful in using the World Wide Web as a primary source of information when they follow a five-step inquiry process that begins with a strategic question and ends with a knowledge product.

Inquiry Process Step One: Framing a Strategic Question

Inquiry-based learning on the web begins with asking or framing a *strategic question*. A strategic question is defined as a question that requires students to make a decision about a course of action (Jakes, 2009). A strategic question enables students to get as much information as possible on their research topic. A knowledge-based or *What is* question is not a strategic question. This type of question calls for a linear response. It takes students from A to B without concern for integrating discrete information pieces into new knowledge or fresh insights (Jakes 2009).

A strategic question, on the other hand, leads to the critical thinking that builds knowledge and links information. Consider the difference in information you can get from a knowledge based question compared to a strategic question across disciplines.

Subject	Example of Knowledge-Based Question	Example of Strategic Question
Health	What is diabetes?	What lifestyle changes can I make to prevent developing diabetes?
Math	What is a geometric shape?	How are geometric shapes used to create building designs?
History	What is a 20th century invention?	What invention of the 20th century has had the greatest impact on 21st century global trade?

Inquiry Process Step Two: Generating Linked Knowledge Questions

The strategic question is important because it frames the research. After the strategic question has been framed, students generate a number of knowledge questions. The answers to factual knowledge questions are the foundation that students use to answer the strategic question. Think about the strategic question for health: *What lifestyle changes can I make to prevent developing diabetes?* Students answer this strategic question by linking information from a number of knowledge questions including *What is diabetes? What are some strategies used to prevent diabetes? What are genetic contributions to diabetes, etc.* Students should be encouraged to develop a list of six to ten knowledge questions and the keywords that will form the basis for answering the strategic question.

The strategic question is important because it frames the research. After the strategic question has been framed, students generate a number of knowledge questions.

Inquiry Process Step Three: Indentifying Keywords

In this step students use the knowledge questions they have written to make a list of key words and phrases. The keywords are used as search tools to access information on the World Wide Web. These key words can be used on search engines, such as Google, Yahoo and AskJeeves. Students should be encouraged to insert quotation marks around phrases in order to narrow their search for more targeted results.

Inquiry Process Step Four: Locating Information and Cross Referencing

Knowledge questions are used in this step to extract information from the World Wide Web. Students must determine what information answers the chain of knowledge questions they have posed and how these answers in turn relate to their overall strategic questions. Students also need to cross reference information from various sites. Middle school and high school students can evaluate the reliability and validity of sites they have chosen to answer their questions. It is through the critical thinking process that students can determine which interdisciplinary facts are most relevant.

Inquiry Step Five: Evaluating Information and Answering the Strategic Question

Finally, students must evaluate whether they have answered all their questions and determine what information they are missing. Once the missing information is retrieved, students must use creative questioning strategies to integrate the data they have found into a fresh insight or a creative solution. The ultimate goal for students is to answer their strategic questions using the knowledge they have gained (Jakes, 2009).

There are a number of web inquiry projects that integrate the steps of generating questions that lead to the answer of a strategic question. Most of these web inquiry projects have a hook that provides the basis for students' inquiry questions. The hook sometimes is a picture, a quote or a video. Students develop strategic inquiry questions based on the hook provided.

Web inquiry projects cross subject disciplines. One history web project focuses on students exploring what it was like to be a young soldier in the Civil War. The web inquiry guides students to a site that has primary source documents including diaries and letters from the Civil War era. The primary documents provide the hook for students to formulate a strategic question and the linked knowledge questions. A list of web-based inquiry sites can be found at the end of this chapter (Davis, 2009).

Web-based Inquiry projects are useful in science and health because they direct students to the most current research on topics being studied (Davis, 2009). Elementary, middle school and high school students can benefit from web based inquiry in studying topics that range from dinosaurs, comets and World War II to natural disasters and the human heart. Students are able to find information from anthropologists, meteorologists, historians and heart surgeons to answer their strategic questions. Web-based inquiry projects combine the critical questioning students need to analyze the data they collect and the creative questioning that leads them to come up with new insights from multiple and competing answers.

There are a number of web inquiry projects that integrate the steps of generating questions that lead to the answer of a strategic question. Most of these web inquiry projects have a hook that provides the basis for students' questions.

Learning to ask strategic questions to access information in nonlinear formats like the World Wide Web is an important skill for 21st century learning. Strategic questioning encourages students to integrate or synthesize knowledge, which is one of the most important skills for the Conceptual Age. Strategic questions form the basis for the investigation of authentic topics across disciplines. Most importantly, as students develop strategic questions, they begin to become independent learners and decision makers.

Questioning and English Language Learners

As English learners develop the ability to ask *What, Where, When* **and** *How,* **they should be challenged to ask increasingly more difficult questions.**

English learners need to learn to ask strategic questions as one of the goals of language learning. However, students who are at the preproduction or early production stages of language learning must start with simple questions. As English learners develop the ability to ask *What, Where, When* and *How,* they should be challenged to ask increasingly more difficult questions. They should be given multiple opportunities to practice asking various types of questions in different contexts. The heuristic function of language must be fostered by the teacher through modeling questioning prompts such as: *What is this _____? What is he/she doing? Where is the_____? Why did the_____?* The following hierarchy is an example of the questions English learners need to be encouraged to ask from the least to the most difficult.

English Learners Ask the Questions

Basic Wh Questions

What is the name of this street?

Where is the science book?

When is he going to lunch?

Choice Questions

Is this a noun or a verb?

Is this the beginning or the end of the book?

W and H Questions

What is the name of the state?

Where is the science vocabulary chart?

Who is the main character?

When did the American Revolution start?

How did they discover the gold in Africa?

"Why" and "How" Higher Order Thinking Questions

Why did the boy make the decision not to fight?

Why do the stars look like they are all the same distance away?

What will happen if we change this variable in the experiment?

How would you feel if you were the last person on Earth?

Embedded Questions

Can you explain why the sun is a star?

Could you tell me the difference in these two solutions to the problem?

Note that questions with modal verbs (e.g., Could you …?–Would you …?) are generally more difficult for English learners than those with simple present, past and future verbs. (Source: MCPS Division of ESOL programs, 2004)

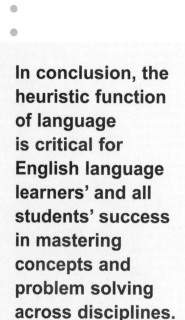

In conclusion, the heuristic function of language is critical for English language learners' and all students' success in mastering concepts and problem solving across disciplines.

In Conclusion

In conclusion, the heuristic function of language is critical for English language learners' and all students' success in mastering concepts and problem solving across disciplines. Questioning is both an intuitive and learned process. It starts as an intuitive process as learners naturally are inquisitive about the world. Questioning then develops as a learned process. The Best Practice Teacher facilitates the process by moving students from asking knowledge-based questions to formulating open-ended strategic critical and creative inquiries.

Many research studies document the teacher's facilitation of students' questioning strategies as a Best Practice. The teacher needs to instruct students in order for them to become proficient in formulating: knowledge-based (what questions), critical thinking (why questions), research (why and apply questions), creative thinking (what if questions) and questions related to nonlinear formats (strategic questions).

Studies show unequivocally that learning to ask these types of questions enhances students' performance across disciplines (Mattheis, 2008). Evidence also suggests that becoming proficient in formulating different types of inquiries enhances students' vocabulary, conceptual understanding of subject content and aids in the construction of logico-mathematical problem solving (Contreras, 2007).

The development of student questioning skills has also been documented to help close the achievement gap when implemented from the onset of schooling (Roseberry, 1990). Learning to formulate questions to find, integrate and apply information develops the academic vocabulary, communication skills, categorization skills, thinking skills and the problem solving strategies needed for academic success.

The Best Practice teacher encourages questioning in the classroom by modeling knowledge-based as well as open-ended critical and creative questioning. The goal is for the Best Practice teacher to facilitate the process of student questioning as an integral part to content instruction across the curriculum.

These are some websites for inquiry based projects:

- http://edweb.sdsu.edu/wip/stages.html

- http:www.biopoint.com/inquiry/ibr.html

- http:lew2.loc.gov/ammem/ndlpedu/lessons/psources/pshome.html

- http://www.gemsvt.org/middle/grade8/socialstudies/geography.htm

(These websites are active as of February, 2009.)

Think About Discussion Questions

1. Think about the process for learning to formulate questions to access information on the World Wide Web outlined on pages 63-65. Choose a topic that relates to the subject area you teach or one of the subject areas you teach. Explain how you will instruct students in the process of creating Strategic questions.

2. Create a chart like the one on page 60 with critical and creative questions related to the subject area you teach or one of the subject areas you teach. Analyze how both types of questions develop students' conceptual understanding of the subject area you have chosen.

Reflection on the Heuristic Function of Language

1. Reflect on the 21st century Conceptual Age. Analyze how you can help students learn the process of strategic questioning in your subject area or in a subject area you teach.

2. Reflect on the English learners in your classroom and the hierarchy of questions for English learners on pages 66-67. Create a graphic organizer with the level of questions that you need to target for the English learners in your classroom.

Chapter 4

Problem Solving

Problem solving across subject disciplines has been for the most part linear moving from step to step. Students have been so busy focusing on details in a straight line A-B-C-D-E , that they have missed the relationships that can be inferred by connecting A to C or maybe C to A in that order.

Reasoning and Problem Solving for the 21st Century Conceptual Age

For nearly a century, Western society in general and the United States in particular have been dominated by a form of thinking and an approach to life that is narrowly linear and deeply analytical. Ours has been the age of the "knowledge worker," a manipulator of information. But that is changing thanks to an array of forces including powerful technologies and globalization. We are entering a new age. It is an age animated by a different type of thinking (Pink, 2006).

Conceptual Age 21st century thinking depends on *infolinking*, creative questioning and open-ended reasoning and problem solving.

Pink describes in his book, *A Whole New Mind*, a seismic change in global thinking that is shifting from the logical, analytic, linear thinking of the 20th century Information Age to the inventive, creative, integrative thinking of the 21st century. The Conceptual Age, according to Pink, necessitates a change in the type of narrowly reductive and deeply analytical thinking that has dominated Western society for decades to a new form of thinking that is based on synthesis and crafting something new through combining seemingly unrelated ideas. Conceptual Age 21st century thinking depends on *infolinking*, creative questioning, open-ended reasoning and problem solving.

The magnitude of this shift in Conceptual Age global thinking can be seen in the changes in businesses and the workforce. Powerful technologies are eliminating or outsourcing the routine jobs of the past and demanding a new type of worker that can think and innovate rather than crank and crunch. While the shift from linear to non linear thinking and problem solving is occurring in business, trades, professions, banking, entertainment, transportation and communication, it has yet to really permeate the K-12 education system.

Analytic and Creative Problem Solving and Education

Problem Solving as it has been implemented for decades in the formal K-12 educational system has emphasized, for the most part, linear, analytic problem solving. Students have been taught how to follow a logical argument, or to figure out linearly the answer to a math or an algebra problem. Students have been encouraged to eliminate incorrect answers and to focus on the one correct response.

The emphasis on linear problem solving and scripted direct instruction texts has left a huge void in concept learning. Students may know how to follow the logical problem solving steps but they often find it difficult to solve problems where there is no one right answer. These same students have not had sufficient opportunity across subject disciplines to engage in the nonlinear problem solving that focuses on exploring ideas and generating possibilities. They have been so busy focusing on details in a straight line 1-2-3-4-5 that they have missed the relationships that can be inferred by connecting 1 to 3 or maybe 3 to 5 in that order.

Students' success in the 21st century requires an expansion of the linear problem solving model. Problem solving needs to become a more nonlinear open, rather than a closed process.

What is Reasoning and Problem Solving?

What is the first thought that comes into your head when you hear the words problem solving? Do you think of the word problems that you attempted to solve in math? Do you see visions of algebraic equations? Do you think of a personal problem? Do you think of a community challenge that must be addressed?

While problem solving is most often related to math, it actually is an activity that crosses subject disciplines.

> **The emphasis on linear problem solving and scripted direct instruction texts has left a huge void in concept learning. Students may know how to follow the logical problem solving steps but they often find it difficult to solve problems where there is no one right answer.**

Problem solving occurs naturally in response to a challenge or problem. The formal definition of a *problem* is a situation, quantitative or otherwise, that requires resolution and for which learners see no apparent or obvious means or path to obtaining a solution (Schrock, 2009). The goal of problem solving is to come up not only with the resolution to a problem but also to explore alternatives. Problem solving has five critical components.

TThe first component is *brainstorming*. Students must identify the problem and come up with possibilities for research topics. The second step is *questioning*. By formulating a series of questions, learners establish the nature of the problem they will address. Next learners must *perceive the problem* as *a challenge* to which they do not have an immediate solution. Then learners must *actively explore the problem in attempting a solution*. Finally, students must consider *alternative solutions*.

These components to problem solving can be noted in the following graphic organizer:

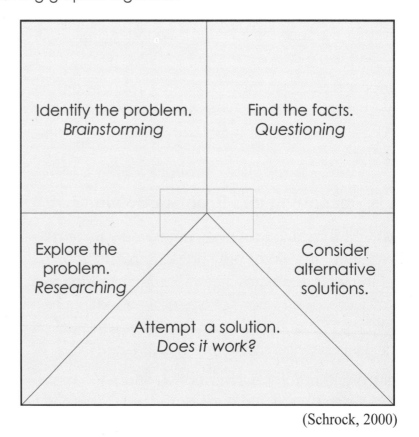

Identify the problem. *Brainstorming*

Find the facts. *Questioning*

Explore the problem. *Researching*

Consider alternative solutions.

Attempt a solution. *Does it work?*

(Schrock, 2000)

The Act of Problem Solving

Learners are natural pattern seekers. They are always trying to make sense of the phenomena they observe and experience. Cognitive theory regards learners as active, not passive problem solvers. They innately interact with the elements from the environment to solve problems. As learners, they use their natural curiosity to make sense of the world around them. Learners form their own theories about the world and the relationships among its different aspects. Their theories may be primitive at first, but eventually the theories become more realistic as they are tested against the learners' experiences.

Students learn about the world by problem solving and the testing of hypotheses. Students learn about history, science, language arts and mathematics in the same way. The importance of reasoning and problem solving across disciplines cannot be overstated. Constructing valid arguments, criticizing, analyzing and creating new insights is integral to the learning process. As students develop their reasoning power, learning becomes more than memorizing facts, mimicking examples or following a rote set of procedures. It becomes a creative process of thinking and reasoning.

There are two broad types of reasoning used in problem solving: inductive and deductive. When students recognize a pattern, formulate a descriptive statement and apply it to a new situation, they are reasoning inductively. When students recognize, state and explain conclusions that follow from their hypotheses, they are reasoning deductively (Intersegmental Committee of the Academic Sciences, 2007).

Problem solving is not taught to students by giving them a set of rules and algorithms to memorize. Students acquire problem-solving skills through the direct experience of exploring and confronting a challenge and by formulating new experiences to find solutions. Students can take on the roles of mathematicians, scientists, social scientists or linguists as they engage in scientific inquiry. As in any inquiry, students need the opportunity to explain their strategies and share their results with peers.

Often in these encounters, students find there is more than one way to solve a problem.

The teacher's role is to guide students in an open environment of authentic inquiry. Research shows that students achieve at higher levels when the teacher creates an authentic environment where students gain the confidence and experience-based skills to find their own solutions to problems. Best Practice teaching across subject areas provides the opportunity for students literally to construct their own understandings.

Teaching Problem Solving as Guided Discovery

How do teachers instruct students in the process of problem solving? They ask questions that guide students to integrate facts and discover new concepts across subject disciplines. Teachers also encourage students to do the following.

- Try and apply a variety of strategies to untangle a problem.

- Design open-ended experiments.

- Organize data on a computer spreadsheet.

- Collect and post data for evaluation by the teacher and peers.

- Have discussions over the results and interpretation of data.

- Explore concepts using visuals, manipulatives and internet links.

- Use nonlinear, open-ended creative thinking.

Open-ended problem solving takes learners from what they know to what is possible. It encourages students to make conjectures and to "think "out-of the-box." Students begin to be in the vanguard. They act like mathematicians, scientists, linguists and historians as they gather relevant facts and explore alternatives.

Problem solving can be promoted across disciplines through two approaches. The first approach is linear in that it takes students through the steps of problem solving. The second approach is the more creative nonlinear problem solving. Students need to be able to use both linear and nonlinear approaches together and interchangeably depending on the nature of the problem (Pink, 2006).

The classic steps to linear problem solving were first outlined by George Polya in 1945. Since then there have been many variations but the steps, for the most part, have remained the same. These include the following:

1. Define the Problem

- *Can you state the problem in your own words?*

- *What are you trying to discover or find out?*

- *What are the unknowns?*

- *What facts and information do you know?*

- *What information, if any, is missing or not needed?*

2. Devise a Plan

- *Examine related problems, and determine if the same technique can be applied.*

- *Examine a simpler or special case of the problem to gain insight into the solution of the original problem.*

- *Make a table or diagram to identify facts and unknowns.*

- *Look for patterns and compare and contrast elements.*

3. Carry out the Plan

- *Implement the strategy or strategies in step 2, and perform any necessary actions or computations.*

- *Check each step of the plan as you proceed.*

- *Keep an accurate record of your work.*

4. Verify Results

- *Interpret the solution in terms of the original problem. Does your answer make sense? Is it reasonable?*

- *Determine whether there is an alternative method of finding the solution.*

- *If possible, determine other related or more general problems for which the techniques will work (Polya, 1945).*

You will notice that this traditional problem solving method has linear steps. Students must complete one task before moving on to the next. The key element is usually critical thinking. This is very different from nonlinear problem solving. Here the imagination is the only limitation. Problem solving is viewed as an artistic endeavor. It is creative thinking that is emphasized. Edward DeBono has a useful five-step process for nonlinear problem-solving:

To   **Where do You Want to Get To? (Definition)**
Lo   **Look at the Problem. (Logical Analysis)**
Po   **Possible Solutions (Generate Possibilities)**
So   **So What Shall We Do? (Make your Decision)**
Go   **Get Going (The Implementation Phase)**

(DeBono, 2007)

The above nonlinear model is very useful when it comes to real-life problems, the sort of problems that have many possible solutions. In the problem-solving process, many students get stuck at the *Possible Solutions PO phase*. They cannot generate a number of possibilities. This may be largely due to an educational system that promotes the one right answer mentality.

Yet, idea generation is a 21st century skill and needs to be cultivated. This *lack of inspiration* can be changed with practice using problems designed to stimulate students' ability to come up with possibilities, Students soon realize there can be many different solutions to a problem, or that there are many ways to tackle a challenge.

Students will discover ultimately on their own that by generating many possible solutions, they can come up with the single possibility that seems most plausible.

Creative thinking using the nonlinear model may be easier for some students than for others. Yet all students can learn this type of thinking. The nonlinear or the lateral thinking that DeBono advocates is a technique designed to help students improve their ability to come up with creative solutions, including those that they might have normally discounted in the past because the possibilities seemed absurd.

The following is an example of a nonlinear problem that encourages lateral, creative nonlinear thinking. A nonlinear problem requires a different approach; you have to think of the answer first, and then figure out or better yet intuit why it fits the facts.

There are 3 tea cups on the tray. Three people take one cup of tea to taste. How can it be that there is one tea cup left on the tray?

This nonlinear tea cup problem has at its root what Daniel Pink calls "Right Brain Rising" (Pink, 2006). He states:

The last few decades have belonged to a certain kind of person with a certain kind of mind- linear thinkers. The future belongs to a very different kind of person with a very different kind of mind-nonlinear creative and pattern recognizers. We are moving from a society built on logical, linear computer-like capabilities of the information age to an economy and a society built on invention, big picture capabilities of what's rising in its place, the Conceptual Age. This age requires a whole new mind (Pink, 2006).

What does this type of thinking mean for educating students in the problem-solving process? It means that we need a model of problem solving that incorporates both linear and nonlinear thinking. While it is true that certain problems really have a single solution and require linear logical thinking, there are many problems that lend themselves well to creative possibility thinking. In fact, the problem solving process for the 21st century should always conclude with the *What If* questions that encourage possibility thinking. It is these *What If* questions that encourage the change process and move students' thinking from the mundane to the possible.

Therefore, a problem-solving method for the 21st century must tie together the best of the linear thinking process with the right brain intuitive creative thinking process. It can be thought of as a circular process with problem solving really never ending. A conclusion is just the jumping off point for more questions and the generation of more ideas. In this way, students learn to feel comfortable with the open-ended *new mind* thinking of the Conceptual Age.

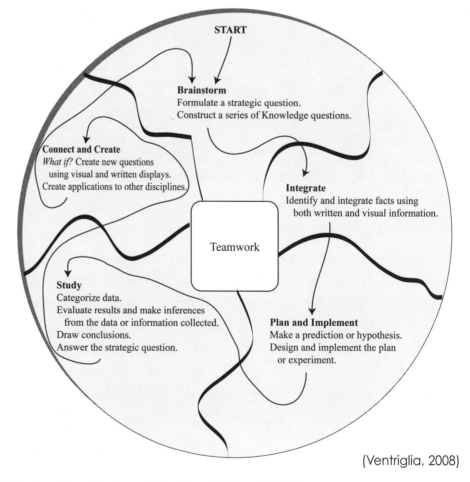

START

Brainstorm
Formulate a strategic question.
Construct a series of Knowledge questions.

Connect and Create
What if? Create new questions
using visual and written displays.
Create applications to other disciplines.

Integrate
Identify and integrate facts using
both written and visual information.

Teamwork

Study
Categorize data.
Evaluate results and make inferences
from the data or information collected.
Draw conclusions.
Answer the strategic question.

Plan and Implement
Make a prediction or hypothesis.
Design and implement the plan
or experiment.

(Ventriglia, 2008)

The implementation of this model starts with brainstorming (a creative process) and ends with *What If* intuitive questions (creative thinking) that lead to a generation of more questions and the process continues. In the middle of the process, students also implement critical thinking. Because the model starts and ends with the creative process it is considered open-ended. This method fits well in the Conceptual Age where change is the only constant (Ventriglia, 2009).

This model can be applied to all subject disciplines. It incorporates the higher level critical and creative thinking processes that are held in common across disciplines. The process of applying increasingly varied and complex thinking processes is one of the ways that students not only sharpen their skills but also strengthen their conceptual understandings.

Think of the subject discipline of mathematics. Research shows unequivocally that the teaching of mathematics should focus on guided problem solving. Yet much of the time in classrooms from first grade through high school instruction is focused on the *how* of mathematical operations, rather than the creative *why* of mathematics. It is certainly true that students need a base in mathematics including mastering number facts before they can leap into problem solving. Yet, many students with this base of knowledge and automaticity in the memory of these facts are still exposed to limited creative problem solving opportunities in which they can apply their mathematical understandings. Authentic open-ended discovery lessons should be part of every classroom. Think of the following story problem as it relates to the 21st century problem solving model.

> *Ants and spiders on the window ledge were*
> *sharing a cup of tea.*
> *An idle question arose that day,*
> *"How many legs are we?"*
> *Forty replied the hungry spiders,*
> *But less than half the legs remained.*
> *The ants took off in such a fright,*
> *Their relationship was strained.*

Students can *brainstorm* together the answer to this problem. They can form a *strategic question* such as *How many ants and spiders were on the window ledge?* They could make a hypothesis or prediction and then set up an equation to solve the problem. After solving the problem, students can ask the *What if* questions to create a new problem such as *What if* the spiders replied "twenty" instead of "forty," etc. They can change the characters in the problem.

You may ask at this point, *What if students can't solve the problem?* If students do not know how to set up equations to solve story problems, of course they need to be taught the math facts and how to set up equations but this is only half of the dilemma. Students then need to be guided to think about not only the *What* but the creative *Why* of mathematics.

In order to guide students in the problem solving process in mathematics, it is important that teachers construct their own mathematical understandings in the same way that students do: by becoming mathematicians and becoming familiar with concepts through direct experience. Improving problem solving in mathematics starts with the teacher's mathematical knowledge (Steffe, 1990). The number one goal of the Mathematics Standards Framework is to:

Increase teachers' knowledge of mathematics content through professional development focusing on standards-based mathematics (Mathematics framework for the California Public Schools, 2000).

How then can the mathematics teacher promote creative problem solving and higher level mathematical thinking? The answer: by extending their knowledge, by interacting with students and by using mathematical thinking to build greater understanding of mathematical ideas. As teachers and students engage in problem solving, opportunities naturally evolve for integrating the 21st century problem solving model that combines critical and creative thinking.

As teachers and students engage in problem solving, opportunities naturally evolve for integrating the 21st century problem solving model that combines critical and creative thinking.

One teacher spoke quite candidly with her students about being a learner in the area of three-dimensional geometry. She built models with her students and struggled alongside them to see objects from different perspectives. In doing so, she opened herself up as a learner to her students. Her students responded with earnest and articulate explanations of their thinking (Mokros, Russell and Economopoulos, 2007).

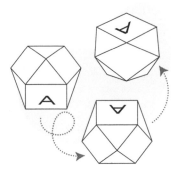

A cuboctahedron being flipped and turned.

Best Practice Problem Solving Strategies for Mathematics

The following Best Practice problem-solving strategies help students apply critical and creative thinking skills to increasingly complex applications of mathematics. These strategies also help students master the mathematical reasoning and problem-solving standards. A thorough understanding of problem solving is not only important in mathematics but needs to be used across subject disciplines.

- **Estimate:** Use approximation or rounding to arrive at a reasonable value or amount by "rough" calculation.

- **Guess and Check:** Use estimation to identify a trial solution. Test the trial solution and revise the estimate. Repeat this sequence until the correct answer is found.

- **Make a Table, Matrix or Chart:** Construct a chart, table, or matrix to organize data for analysis.

- **Make a List:** Use a linear format to organize data by numerical value, ranking, alphabetical order, or other criteria of priority.

- **Look for a Pattern:** Use organized data (linear, matrices, charts, or tables) to identify or deduce inherent trends, patterns, rules, or generalizations.

Model the Problem: Use concrete objects, draw pictures, construct diagrams, or use other representations to visualize relationships and to clarify the task.

Logical Reasoning: Use sound processes of thinking to determine a practical plan for finding the solution. (This strategy may involve the combined use of several other strategies from this list.)

Determine the Facts: Identify the essential data needed to solve the problem. Eliminate unnecessary facts. Use logical reasoning to supply any missing data needed to find a solution.

Choose the Operation: Analyze the problem and data to determine the appropriate operation or operations for finding the solution.

Construct an Equation: Use the data to organize an abstract representation of the problem. (Prerequisite to this are the skills of determining the facts and choosing the operation.)

Work Backwards: Use known data to work back toward the beginning of the problem to understand the process, then apply these understandings to move forward from the known data to the solution of the whole problem.

Simplify the Problem: Solve a similar, easier (less complex) problem to understand the process, then apply those understandings to solve a more complex problem.

Act out the Problem: Reenact the problem kinesthetically. "Going through" the steps, physically modeling the problem, may provide insights that are not obvious in a static format.

Incorporate technology where applicable: Use technology as an aid in calculation to leave more time for concept building.

Inquiry Across Disciplines

Students grow as mathematicians and increase their appreciation of the nature of mathematics as they engage in multiple opportunities to explore mathematical situations both linearly and creatively. If students are "equipped" with effective 21st century inquiry strategies and if they are taught to apply these strategies to the solutions to problems, they start to behave like mathematicians and scientists who form hypotheses and then discover answers" (Mathematics Framework for the California Public Schools, 2000). Students need to apply the strategies of 21st century inquiry across subject disciplines.

The inquiry method in science lends itself well to a 21st century problem solving model. The first step of inquiry involves students in *brainstorming* and establishing a *strategic question or series of questions*. The use of *strategic here* is important because a *strategic question* is higher level and allows for exploring ideas. Students then *construct hypotheses, design experiments, make inferences* and *make connections*. Notice the added last step of making connections and finding alternatives using visual and written displays. These are the *What if* questions that promote rearranging facts to come up with alternative ideas and new possibilities. The Science Framework states the following:

Scientific progress is made by asking meaningful questions and conducting careful investigations. As a basis for understanding this concept and addressing the content students should perform investigations and develop their own problem solving questions (California Science Content Standards, 2000).

The following scenario is an implementation of this model in the classroom setting:

Mrs. Dora Velaz is teaching the 5th grade science standard: The solar system consists of planets and other bodies that orbit the sun. Mrs. Velaz focuses on the sun, which is the largest body in our solar system, as a star. Then she takes students through a brainstorming process to find

These are the *What if* questions that promote rearranging facts to come up with alternative ideas and new possibilities.

out what they know about stars. She asks: What are stars? Students offer responses such as, "They are points of light in the night sky. Stars exist side by side in the sky." Mrs.Velaz writes all students' responses on a whiteboard. Then she leads students to do research on the Internet to find information about the Knowledge questions they asked about stars. She warns students not to answer their questions with the first bit of information they find but instead to rely on multiple sources. She guides students through the digital ocean of information. She helps them develop critical thinking skills to select reliable information. She leads them to Internet visuals of the night sky. Based on what they learned, students formulate the strategic question: Can stars be different distances away and still appear to be side by side? Students are encouraged to make a hypotheses or prediction. Then students engage in an experiment in cooperative groups. Students design a model "star outline" with one star in each corner. The stars are group members holding flashlights. Students with flashlights change positions. Students draw outlines of what they see. Ultimately, students use the results of the experiment to answer the strategic question. But the lesson does not stop here. Mrs. Velaz encourages students in groups to create a series of what if questions. Students are also encouraged to apply what they learned in science to their literature unit on astronomy.

The inquiry embedded in the 21st century model involves students in implementing the critical thinking skills of *observing, categorizing, communicating, inferring* and *drawing conclusions.* Elementary school students observe using their five senses to find out information about stars; *categorize characteristics, like shape, size and distance; infer distance using outlines; communicate and share* ideas with peers; and *infer and draw conclusions about results.* Finally, students are prompted to ask the nonlinear What if questions. What if our universe did not have stars? What if the sun fell out of the sky? Answers to these questions lead to the generation of new questions which in turn start the problem solving process all over again.

This same inquiry model can be used for high school and middle school students with a variety of science topics. Students can brainstorm, formulate *strategic questions,* explore information using multimedia, identify variables and interpret data. Then they can use *What if* questions to extend what they have learned to expand their scientific investigations. Once students have mastered the inquiry model, it can be applied in different ways to other subject disciplines.

Case Studies for Problem Solving in Social Science

The National Council for Social Studies (2000) has identified the Case Study Model as one of the ways to engage students in creative higher level thinking and expand their deep knowledge about social studies (Newby, 2005). An extension of the model is termed the *Case Study Service Model* which incorporates inquiry with community service. Using this model, students research a topic of historical significance and also determine a service outcome for their research.

Problem Solving in the *Case Study Service Model* begins with brainstorming a topic that has relevance to the community. Students work in teams to gather information on a topic such as historic sites in the community that need refurbishing. They use MapQuests and other resources to find out all they can about these historic sites. Students take a field trip or a virtual tour through their local community to observe and visit historical sites, including museums, libraries, and even graveyards.

After returning to the classroom, teachers engage students in an activity where they *list, group and label* what they saw (Zemmelman, 1993). Students then join cooperative groups to formulate a *strategic historical question* and a *strategic service question.* An example of a *strategic* historical question is: *How has the old community graveyard changed over time?* A strategic service question would be: *How can we improve the appearance of this historic site for the community?*

Problem Solving in the *Case Study Service Model* **begins with brainstorming a topic that has relevance to the community. Students work in teams to gather information on a topic such as historic sites in the community that need refurbishing.**

Students answer the historical question by using data collection sources such as primary and secondary documents, interviews, information found on websites, photographs, and on-site visits. Analyzing and interpreting the collected data occurs through substantive conversations and interviews. Students might interview community members who have relatives buried in the graveyard. They might want to record the background of the historic site.

Students *integrate* the information and present their findings through graphic organizers, timelines, graphs, pictures, maps, copies of primary documents, narratives, and computer applications (Newby, 2005). They include a narrative that answers the strategic questions along with discussions of at least three data collection methods. They *evaluate* the collected data. They make recommendations for a service project. They engage in creative thinking to explore *What if* scenarios on getting community members involved in the project. In this way, students learn how to research information like a historian and also apply what they learned to design a community service project.

The Case Study Service Model can also target problem solving to multicultural issues. This method can be used to address instances of cultural conflict at school or in the community. The teacher engages students by having them brainstorm cultural incidents they have witnessed at school. Students can even do short write ups or quick writes and share them through a brainstorming process.

Students work in groups to formulate a strategic question related to the cultural conflict. They research facts including research of similar incidents that may be recorded on the World Wide Web. They check the reliability of Internet sources to make sure they are reading facts and not opinions. Then they integrate the information to devise a solution that may be of service to the school community. The plan is reached by consensus building. Students make inferences on the results of their plan. Then they create a series of *What If* statements that offer at least two other alternative plans. Students continue to think about how they can involve the school community in their plan.

The Case Study Service Model encourages dialogue. It helps students solve problems through critical and creative thinking. Students develop the 21st century skill of consensus building. Students are encouraged to think outside the box. The teacher can build further understanding of problem solving by asking the following questions on the process:

1. *How was the process of using a case study in order to solve the problem helpful?*

2. *How was the process of addressing this case through the collaborative process different?*

3. *What was the most difficult part of participating in this process?*

4. *Of the alternative solutions that were shared perspectives, which ones would you not have considered?*

The inquiry method used in science and social studies can be extended to language arts. Students can use the inquiry method to analyze literature or connect with others in the global community.

Language Arts and Problem Solving

Problem solving in language arts can begin at the kindergarten level. The teacher may use a literature selection to instruct students in the four steps of problem solving :

1. Brainstorm: Identify the problem

2. Ask the Question (Strategic Question)

3. Generate ideas

4. Suggest and Evaluate Solutions

A multicultural, multilingual literature selection like the *Little Red Hen* can be used to teach problem solving at the kindergarten level. The teacher begins the lesson by brainstorming. She or he asks: *Do you ever need help doing something? What do you do to get someone to help you?* Feedback of students is used to engage them in a dialogue. Then the teacher reads the story. *W* questions and *How* questions are asked throughout the reading.

After the reading, the teacher guides students through the problem-solving process. Students *identify* the problem of the red hen. The teacher helps students formulate or *ask* a strategic question like: *How can the red hen get help to make the bread?* Students *generate ideas*. Finally, students *suggest* and *evaluate solutions* to the hen's dilemma that work better than baking the bread herself. In this way, students begin to learn the process of problem solving.

Problem solving at the middle school and high school level can address the English language arts standard: *Write job applications and resumes*. A unit on careers can draw students into learning the problem-solving skills that are important to succeed in many careers. Students first formulate *strategic* questions such as: *What occupations will be growing in the 21st century? What problem-solving skills does a person need to perform these jobs?* Working in pairs, students can use the various sources on the Internet as well as occupational printouts from the Department of Labor to find 21st century occupations that are growing. They then choose a job they are interested in and explore how this profession uses problem-solving skills to perform the job. Students can organize the information they found on a graphic organizer.

Project-based learning can also be used with the 21st century inquiry method. In her book *Virtual Architecture,* Harris (1998) gives a number of examples of projects where problem solving is used with multimedia applications.

Project-based learning can also be used with the 21st century inquiry method. In her book *Virtual Architecture,* Harris (1998) gives a number of examples of projects where problem solving is used with multimedia applications. Projects like *YouthCAN*, a youth-run site, use technology to connect and help people around the globe learn about environmental issues. Peers can formulate strategic questions and devise solutions cross continentally for global issues. Online simulation gives students the opportunity to communicate electronically about issues related to the protection of fundamental liberties, freedoms and human rights while also examining national security issues. Another site for elementary learners involves students in problem solving to test different stain removers. There is an online form where students can record ways to get rid of mustard, ink and other substances (Harris, 1998).

Choosing and Constructing Interdisciplinary Problem Solving

Students grow in their appreciation for the inquiry process when they engage in multiple opportunities to explore problem solving across disciplines. If students are equipped with effective problem-solving strategies and are taught to apply these strategies to interdisciplinary problems, they become prepared to function in the 21st century Conceptual Age (Pink, 2006).

In designing and selecting opportunities to implement the 21st century problem-solving model, the goal is to maximize the time spent on the inquiry process. There are many potentially "good" problem-solving activities. However, there are many levels at which a problem is or is not good with criteria ranging from the practical to the creative. Effective problem-solving activities need to include elements that lend themselves to both critical and creative thinking. While some problem-solving activities require a right answer, others extend learning from that point to alternative solutions that require creative thinking. These are the type of activities that should be included in the 21st century classroom.

Best Practice teachers looking for good problem solving activities need to ask the following questions:

- *Does the solving of this problem lead to further understanding of subject concepts or interdisciplinary concepts, ideas and relationships?*

- *Does this problem-solving activity lead students to consider important ideas that reach beyond the particular solution or result? Are there different ways into the problem so that students with different strengths, needs and experiences are able to engage in some aspects of the problem?*

- *Is the problem interesting to a wide range of students? (Mokros et al., 2007)*

- *As students become involved in the problem, are they grabbed by the possibilities of alternate solutions that they can create?*

> **In designing and selecting opportunities to implement the 21st century problem-solving model, the goal is to maximize the time spent on the inquiry process.**

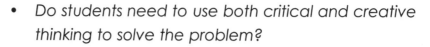

- *Do students need to use both critical and creative thinking to solve the problem?*

- *Does the problem provide direction and structure without overly limiting the ways in which students might solve the problem creatively?*

- *Does the problem include both linear and nonlinear thinking aspects?*

In Conclusion

It is absolutely important and necessary for teachers themselves to become involved in the problem-solving process. Teachers along with students need to stretch their thinking from the linear to the creative nonlinear thinking process.

The most important job facing teachers whose students will spend their lives in the 21st century is to teach them *strategic* questioning and problem-solving skills (Steffe, 2006). Teachers need to adopt the belief that problem solving is an essential human activity and that meaning is created across subject areas through inquiry activities. Best Practice teaching diminishes the linear approach to inquiry that demands one right answer and extends problem solving to open-ended opportunities that enrich students' daily lives.

Best Practice teaching seeks to encourage students to find alternative solutions to real world problems. Solving 21st century problems often requires the use of multimedia applications. Students need to learn how to surf the Internet strategically as they solve problems. This includes distinguishing between reliable and unreliable sources. Once reliable sources have been found, students must be instructed on how to use the information to justify their thinking and conclusions. Finally, students must be taught that problem solving is a never ending process. A solution today is outdated tomorrow. This is the reality of the 21st century. Best Practice teachers, by taking students through problem solving as a discovery process, help students achieve a good balance between critical and creative thinking.

Think About Discussion Questions

1. Think about the 21st century circular problem-solving model on page 80. Describe how you can apply this model to the subject area or one of the subject areas you teach.

2. Compare and contrast on a graphic organizer linear and nonlinear problem solving as described in this chapter. Evaluate the value of linear and nonlinear problem solving in the subject area you teach or in one of the subject areas you teach.

Reflection on 21st Century Problem Solving

1. Reflect on the 21st century problem solving model. What are the limitations of the model for students that have not mastered foundational skills in a subject area? Analyze how you can involve these students in some aspects of problem solving through cooperative learning activities.

2. Reflect on the limitations of using only digital or text information for problem solving?

Chapter 5

Communicating and Applying Knowledge in the 21st Century Classroom

There are a number of activities that engage students in communicating and applying knowledge in the 21st century classroom. These include written communication, Story, visual communication, Design, spatial activities, applications using diverse forms of technology and authentic experiences that have global applications.

The Art of 21st Century Communication

Facts in the 21st century will continue to become widely available and instantly accessible. The goal of the 21st century learner will be to take these facts, put them together and present them meaningfully through oral, written and visual communication.

The "art of communication" in the 21st century classroom motivates students to creatively manipulate data and apply knowledge in a new way to answer a strategic question or to solve a global problem. Creative 21st century communication is facilitated through students' engagement in dialogues and powerful conversations.

Why aren't students across subject areas encouraged to have conversations? What better way is there to test theories and ideas than sharing hunches with a partner? According to experts, 80% of the day is spent on conversations in the workforce (James, 2009). Yet, 10% or less of the day is spent on student conversations in most classrooms (Kremer, 2007). This is especially true in mathematics classrooms. Students are encouraged to work independently and rarely problem solve and have meaningful conversations with their peers. This is despite the fact that the study of mathematics and all subject areas involves problem solving.

Sharing ideas through conversations is what workers do. Construction workers don't erect a building in silence or isolation. You hear the sounds of their tools and conversations back and forth as they ask for materials, seek advice, ask for validation from blueprints or request assistance in moving and positioning heavy beams.

Mathematicians, scientists, historians and linguists share insights as they work collaboratively on mathematical, scientific or social problems. They do not work without talking or in isolation. They converse about and cooperate to untangle confusing aspects of a problem. They clarify parameters and sometimes argue about the most effective strategies to solve a problem.

> **The "art of communication" in the 21st century classroom motivates students to creatively manipulate data and apply knowledge in a new way to answer a strategic question or to solve a real world problem. Creative 21st century communication is facilitated through students' engagement in dialogues and powerful conversations.**

Just as workers use conversations to share insights on problem solving, students need to be encouraged to have conversations. Conversing and interacting with classmates allows students to make sense of the facts and concepts they are learning. Student interactions maximize their opportunities to get immediate feedback. They have the opportunity to evaluate solutions to problems and adjust their problem solving strategies. They come to realize that learning can be viewed from multiple perspectives which may include cultural aspects.

Communication is essential for learning. There are multiple ways to use communication to foster learning in the 21st century classroom. These include effective discussions, interdisciplinary communication, narratives (Story), visuals (Design), and Information and Communication Technology (ICT) literacy.

Oral Communication: Effective Discussions

Teachers play an important role in promoting effective classroom discussions. It is important that the teacher model how to listen, question, reason, be engaged in a discussion, and be an effective audience for another's work (Mokros, Russell, Economopoulos, 2007).

Effective discussions involve students in articulating the purpose for what they are learning, the logic of their problem-solving procedures and the reasonableness of their solutions. When students are asked to orally explain their thinking, they are forced to organize their ideas. They have the opportunity to develop, cement and extend their understanding (Kremer, 2007).

It is critical for students to have a forum for their ideas. Discussions with their peers help students organize their thoughts and consider diverse viewpoints. It is through the examination of multiple perspectives that problems are most creatively solved.

Communication is essential for learning. There are multiple ways to use communication to foster learning in the 21st century classroom. These include effective discussions, interdisciplinary communication, narratives (Story), visuals (Design), and Information and Communication Technology (ICT) literacy.

Students can share their ideas with a partner or in cooperative learning groups. The key is that they share their ideas, rather than invent in a vacuum. Working in teams is part of 21st century communication across workforce professions. Students prepare for their future roles by learning to work with others. Though students may not agree with their peers, they nonetheless come to realize that there are multiple ways to arrive at a solution. This is an important 21st century skill. All knowledge in the 21st century is increasingly considered multidimensional rather than one dimensional. Students must learn the flexibility required to work and live in a world that continues to see knowledge as multifaceted and temporary rather than fixed and unchangeable (Mokros, Russell, Economopoulos, 2007).

All knowledge in the 21st century is increasingly considered multidimensional rather than one dimensional.

Students need extensive experience in oral communication. They need constructive and detailed oral feedback. Students need to become comfortable with the language of mathematics, science, social science, language arts and any other discipline they are studying. The goal is for students to develop an extensive interdisciplinary vocabulary so that they can easily discuss issues across subject disciplines. The preciseness of students' communication in each subject area contributes to the effectiveness of their cross curricular reasoning in the problem solving process (Intersegmental Committee of the Academic Sciences, 2007).

Interdisciplinary Communication

Students not only need the vocabulary of each subject, they also need the interdisciplinary vocabulary that enables them to communicate across disciplines. Students can use their interdisciplinary vocabulary base to take creative leaps. They can use terms in a new way to describe a process or idea. It is the act of labeling a new idea that gives it birth. The following is an example of how a new term can be created through active discussion.

Mr. Ron Kremer was accustomed to working with his students in the problem-solving process. One afternoon, he was facilitating an experiment in geometry.

Students were trying to put all their data in a linear sequence, but they were unable to do so. Students began asking each other open-ended What if questions. Students began to order the data they could. They still had three or four solutions left over. So they just tacked on the short sequences where there was a related solution, forming little branches sticking out of the line. As they discussed the solution with each other and the teacher, they decided to label their solution a branching sequence. Sometime later, when Mr. Kremer was writing up the experiment for a geometry book, he used the invented term to describe the students' results. Mr. Kremer did not know the impact of his students' discovery until he saw the advertisement for his geometry book which read: Students create linear and branching sequences (Kremer, 2007).

This example demonstrates the power of a label or word to describe a new way of thinking. This type of thinking will become more prevalent in the 21st century as students work in teams to use facts and concepts to create new understandings. The use of communication to problem solve and synthesize meaning can be facilitated through "A Challenge Board" and through the 21st century technique of "Story" (Pink, 2006).

Challenge Boards

A *Challenge Board*, as its name implies, is used for students to present problems and challenges to their classmates. A Challenge Board can be used across subject areas. It can either be a physical place in a classroom or a website where students post data and questions on a problem. The Challenge Board is meant as a focal point for discussion; it's a place where students get feedback from their peers on the work they've performed. Once students post their data, they work together to review it, answer questions and form generalizations. These generalizations can be used to formulate rules that can be tested against the posted data. Posting and communicating is a form of oral communication that helps students to form communities of mathematicians, scientists, social scientists and authors.

A *Challenge Board*, as its name implies, is used for students to present problems and challenges to their classmates. A Challenge Board can be used across subject areas.

It also prepares them for a 21st century workforce where the posting of global information through technological sources will become more and more prevalent. Students need to learn how to sift through responses and utilize those that reflect a solid knowledge base.

Students can post a paragraph that they need help in editing. They can post the facts that they have found through a science experiment. They can post a community challenge they need help in solving. Questions posted as creative challenges can lead to classroom discussions and then be extended to global communication by email, texting and other new communication tools.

Maria Cuadras, a fifth grader, is working on a draft of her persuasive essay. She is not sure how to convince someone to buy the product she hypothetically is selling. She posts the issue on the challenge board. Soon two or three students come to her aid and through brainstorming with them she is able to formulate an effective argument.

Don Bonner is a high school student working on an algebra problem. He gets stuck at one point. He posts his challenge on a challenge website and soon he gets help in figuring out the part of the problem that he did not understand. The problem may be explained to the student by another student through the use of the technique called Story

Story and 21st Century Oral Communication

In his book *A Whole New Mind*, Pink (2006) refers to the technique he calls *Story*. He claims that it is through narrative imagining that we remember something. He states that the ubiquitous number of facts in the 21st century will make them less valuable. Contrarily, what will become more valuable is the ability to put these facts in a context and deliver them with emotional impact (Pink, 2006).

Story telling has long been a tradition of many cultures. Stories were told to explain physical phenomena as well as to teach certain truths and cultural values. Stories are easier to remember because they are *how we remember* (Pink, 2006).

We remember things when they are connected rather than disconnected. Most of our thinking and knowledge has always been organized in stories. Everything from the biblical gospels to alien sightings has been told in stories. Schank (2008), a cognitive scientist, states *Humans are not set up to understand logic; they are ideally set up to understand stories.* Deming (1990), the author of the continuous improvement model, stated that he learned more from the stories businesses told in the cafeteria than from their official bank documents.

Stories are important cognitive events for they encapsulate in one compact package, information, knowledge, context and emotion (Pink, 2006). According to Pink, stories are extremely valuable in the 21st century Conceptual Age.

The question is what is the purpose of stories in the 21st century classroom? The creation of stories to explain math concepts, historical events or personal challenges develops one of the key skills for the 21st century which is *synthesis*. Synthesis is the skill of taking facts and integrating them into a context to create meaning. This skill is particularly important in 21st century interdisciplinary learning. Learning is not solidified by analyzing facts from each discipline. Isolated facts from each subject discipline are not easily remembered. What is remembered is a new pattern or a new way of thinking students create by putting together interdisciplinary facts that no one has thought about putting together before.

Stories are important cognitive events for they encapsulate in one compact package, information, knowledge, context and emotion (Pink, 2006).

Once students have integrated facts across disciplines, they can create a narrative to draw others into their thinking. The teacher encourages students to tell their classmates what they learned in the form of a *Story*. Students who put together what they learned in a created *Story* not only remember the facts, they get practice using the powerful skill of synthesis.

The technique of Story can be used to teach subject standards through an interdisciplinary theme. The following 8th grade subject standards and activities are used to teach the interdisciplinary theme entitled *Artificial Environments and Man's Manipulation of the Life Space*.

Then the technique of Story is used to tie together what students have learned. The lesson presentation starts with the introduction of the following interdisciplinary standards.

Social Science: *Discuss the influence of industrialization and technological developments on the region, including human modification of the landscape.*

English Language Arts: *Know words derived from Greek and Latin roots.*

Mathematics: *Students use and know simple aspects of a logical argument.*

Students apply the standards in these activities:

1. Research the history of man's inventions and the application of these social artifacts to diverse tasks. (social science)

2. Students will do historical research. (social science)

3. The important scientific principles that formed the basis of inventions through time. (science)

4. Construct charts and graphs on population changes and effects on the environment. (mathematics)

5. Tell the story. (language arts)

This excerpt is an example of how *Story* can be created as a synthesis of what students learned in the unit.

The clock is ticking. I move the hands backwards, backwards, backwards, to the earliest times of Man. I see myself as part of the earliest society. Our community is struggling to conquer nature. We are trying hard to dominate our surroundings. We have plowed the land. We have constructed crude instruments to use for hunting. The clock keeps ticking faster and faster. We are progressing faster and faster. We are riding in a horse and buggy down a dark dirt road. We pass farmhouses with candles in their windows. Suddenly the clock advances and we are driving in a luxury vehicle past skyscrapers, our roads are paved, electricity lights the road. Everywhere, things keep changing—everywhere—all in Man's attempt to reconfigure the character of our global lifespace in his and her image.

In this example, the technique of Story was used to recreate and synthesize the facts. The creativity fostered by this technique is evidenced by the use of the clock moving backward and then forward to the present time. Students who create their own stories reinterpret the facts in a personal way. Students remember the facts because they have created the *Story*.

21st Century Written Communication: My Thinking Journal

Written communication in the 21st century classroom is used not only for research reports and written subject area assignments, it is utilized to have students revisit and reflect on their thinking. It is a strategy for understanding. Written communication is seen in the classroom as an interdisciplinary activity. Students do not only write in the language arts and history block, they also write in math and science. Creative notetaking is a 21st century skill that is important across subject disciplines. When students take notes, they use the skill of synthesis to integrate information in short segments that will help them remember facts and concepts. Teachers can facilitate the process of creative notetaking by giving students notebooks that they can use during direct instruction to write notes and questions they may have about the lesson. Teachers can instruct students on how to take notes efficiently and effectively. Creative notetaking implies that students may use words or visuals to synthesize information.

Mr. Victor Martinez is teaching his students how to take notes. He tells them to:

- Write on one side of the sheet of paper only or in the margins of the book if permissable.

- Write or illustrate the big ideas (You may want to write down the page from the text.)

- Use diagrams to show connections between ideas.

- Use abbreviations and symbols "Never use a sentence when you can use a phrase, or a phrase when you can use a word" (Berkeley, 2007).

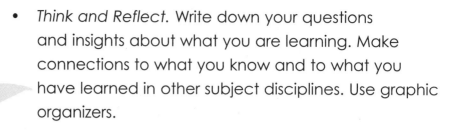

- *Think and Reflect.* Write down your questions and insights about what you are learning. Make connections to what you know and to what you have learned in other subject disciplines. Use graphic organizers.

- Write all unfamiliar vocabulary words so you can look them up later.

Notetaking as written communication extends to the use of *My Thinking Journals.* Students use these journals to record their thinking about a subject or idea that they learned. They can also share their thoughts with a partner. The partner can ask clarification questions. Having journals in which they can record their thoughts is very important for 21st century learners. The same journals can be used throughout the day. At the end of the day, students can be asked to integrate their thoughts across disciplines in one central idea. Most importantly they can be asked how they can apply what they learned across subject areas and in their daily lives. Writing down thoughts leads to the important 21st century skill of formulating insights and taking cognitive leaps from what is to what could be.

My Thinking Journal   January 30_____

Today, I thought about what we learned in science class about genetic engineering. Scientists have recently developed a new method of controlling inherited traits of offspring. What if everyone in the world wanted the same traits? Would this change society as we know it? What if everyone were blond with blue eyes? Is moving genes from one organism to another really a good idea for society?????

This excerpt shows how Thinking Journals involve students in asking the *What If* questions that are so important in the 21st century. It also manifests how students move from the study of science to social science and philosophy as they question the ethics of genetic engineering. Thinking journals can also include visual representations of thinking.

21st Century Visual Communication: Design

Have you ever heard the expression "a picture is worth a thousand words"? Visual communication is important in the 21st century Conceptual Age. It is a right-brained activity. Pink (2006) refers to visual communication as *Design*. He states that Design is a whole-minded aptitude. Because technology has made design accessible to everyone, it can be used to portray all kinds of thoughts. It is another method that relies on synthesis. It is the synthesis of taking ideas and putting them in the visual form. It also is a means to capture thoughts that are difficult to express in a linear written format.

It is important that students use this right brain skill in 21st century classrooms both to portray knowledge and to create new insights—even ideas that change the world. The teacher in the 21st century classroom should use *Design* to teach all core academic subjects. *Design* is interdisciplinary. It also marries the left and right hemisphere. It creates students who can think holistically (Pink, 2006).

Think of a history class. Instead of talking about how pyramids were created, students can actually build a pyramid. In math, instead of talking about spatial skills in geometry, students can experience these skills by actually creating designs. The following is an example from mathematics.

Mrs. Jane Saaman was exploring a group of polyominoes called pentominoes *with her class. The students were investigating the question: How many different ways can you arrange five squares? (The only constants were that every square must share one edge with another square, and no square could touch at a vertex only.)*

The students were creating designs of pasted squares on paper to record their solutions. The students cut the patterns out and put them in the data collection box. After the students had an opportunity to explore the question and add their solution to the data collection, the box was emptied and the design solutions were posted on a large bulletin board.

The students evaluated the posted data by looking for duplicates and removing them from the board. Often students came up to the board, took a solution down, then tried to flip or rotate it to see if it physically covered another solution on the board. (If it was a duplicate, the solution was set aside.) After a while, when the teacher was facilitating by standing at the board and removing duplicates, he noticed that a number of students were able to flip or rotate solutions mentally without actually going up to the board. In a fairly short period of time, the students became proficient at several spatial visualization skills (Kremer, 2007).

On another occasion, the same class spent considerable time building models of geometric solids. They had begun first by observing and drawing several types of crystals using simple microscopes, and then building models of them using soda straws and scotch tape. Later they began building other models (pyramids, prisms, etc.) using commercial construction sets. As they analyzed and compared the models, counting edges, faces and vertices, the students were able to manipulate the three-dimensional constructions with ease. Several adults observing the students' intensity were surprised by their willingness to tackle even more complex solids (Kremer, 2007).

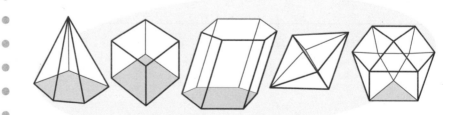

Students also can use the 21st century skill of *Design* to visually represent science and math concepts by creating concrete models. Appropriate models may be concrete or representational (using diagrams, drawings or visual models).

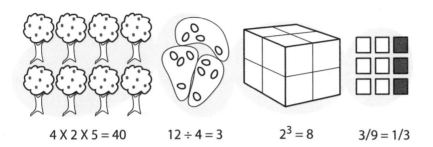

$$4 \times 2 \times 5 = 40 \qquad 12 \div 4 = 3 \qquad 2^3 = 8 \qquad 3/9 = 1/3$$

The skill of *Design* lends itself well to interdisciplinary instruction. Students can use models in science, social science, health and mathematics to represent complex relationships. In the examples above, the relationships are geometric in nature. The trees and boxes are arrays or matrices. The cube is a three-dimensional matrix. Students who may not feel confident in arithmetic may have good spatial skills (concrete and manipulative). Modeling enables these students to make sense of complex mathematical ideas as they change abstract concepts into concrete relationships that can be visually analyzed and compared (Kremer, 2007).

The use of Design to create models of ideas requires the important skill of synthesis. Students have to integrate a number of elements to come up with a visual representation of a concept. Students who are able to construct both written and physical models will have an advantage over other learners in the 21st century (Mokros, Russell, and Economopoulos, 2007).

Whiteboards can be used across subject disciplines to have students use *Design* to create a visual to express their understanding of a subject concept. The teacher may be explaining a science standard that addresses the position of the Earth in relation to other planets. This is a perfect time for students to draw on their whiteboards the concept that is being discussed.

If the teacher is discussing the *underground railroad* in social science, this is the perfect opportunity for students to draw their understanding of the underground railroad. They can also draw out positions in football as well as notes in music that go with a song. There are a number of ways in mathematics to have students use Design to express their mathematical understandings.

Place Value: The teacher says: *Write the number I say using numerals,"* or *"Write the number I say using words.* (Previous to this activity you may wish to use the white boards for an informal spelling test of words that name numerals, like "twelve" or "thousand," etc.)

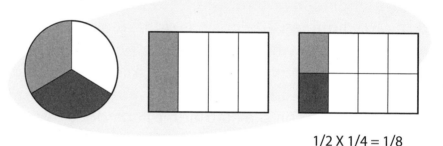

$$1/2 \times 1/4 = 1/8$$

Fractions: The teacher says: *Draw a picture of 2/3rds. Draw a rectangle and divide it into fourths by making four vertical columns. Shade in one fourth of the rectangle, (one column). Now draw a horizontal line, dividing the rectangle in half. Fill in one half of the shaded column. Beneath the drawing, write a number sentence describing what you did. Write a story problem for each of the fractions.*

Geometry: The teacher says: *Draw a pentagon. Use your straight edge and protractor to construct any triangle. Use the classification chart in your book to identify and label your triangle according to its angles. Or label your triangle according to its sides.*

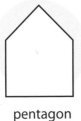

pentagon

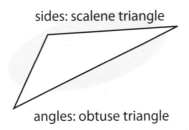

sides: scalene triangle

angles: obtuse triangle

Measurement: The teacher says: *Use your ruler to draw a line four inches long. Mark off the inches on your line. Trade white boards with your neighbor and*

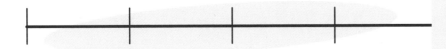

remeasure their line to check it.

At the end of each response, students show their whiteboards to the teacher. Students may be asked to confer with a peer before holding up their responses. The teacher must be alert when using this process to students who may be so unsure of their answers that they may be sensitive to peer review.

Show each other: compare

Show the teacher

The use of *Design* throughout the day enhances students' ability to show conceptual understandings. Visuals can represent generalizations and patterns.

Connecting and Applying Through Design

Representing fractions and other mathematics concepts is an elementary form of the use of visuals. Design can be extended to have students visually create patterns and interdisciplinary connections. For example, students who are studying snowflakes in science may be asked to create visually as many connections as possible between snowflakes and mathematics.

Students can also make representations of patterns, trends and generalizations from history or health science. The use of Design throughout the day enhances students' ability to show conceptual understandings. Visuals can represent generalizations and patterns. The combination of written communication and visual communication leads to creative insights. This combination of skills prepares students to be successful in the Conceptual Age.

Information and Communication Technology (ICT) Literacy

In order to succeed in the 21st century, students must master the ability to use appropriate technologies to process, analyze and present information efficiently and effectively in school, life and work settings. Virtual school settings require students to master technology as part of their everyday learning. Students are able to refine their technology skills. Students become adept at the skills they need to participate in the global, web-driven world (NACOL, 2009).

All students should be exposed to both on ground and web-based learning to develop their communication skills and problem solving skills. For example, students can use written and visual communication or Design in a web-based geometry program that has them share digital blueprints. They can learn about shapes from surveying local buildings online.

The only limitation to 21st century learning is truly the imagination. The Best Practice teacher considers learning as a multidimensional activity. He or she uses Oral and Written Communication, Narratives (Story), Visual Communication (Design) and Information and communication (ICT) literacy to create the optimum classroom environment.

Think About Discussion Questions

1. Think about the concept of *Story* (Pink, 2006) as a synthesis technique. Write an activity to show how you could apply this technique in your classroom.

2. Think about the subject or subjects you teach. Evaluate the percentage of time you spend on written versus visual communication to teach the content standards.

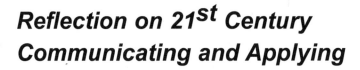

Reflection on 21st Century Communicating and Applying

1. Reflect upon how you can foster more visual communication in the subject area or subject areas you teach.

2. Reflect upon the oral communication in your classroom. Evaluate the effectiveness of your classroom discussion in encouraging students' thinking about what they are learning. Use a scale from one to ten.

Chapter 6

Teaching to the 21st Century Standards

How can students master standards if they don't have the opportunity to learn and practice them?

Content Standards Guide Teaching and Learning

What is a standard? A standard is defined in the dictionary as:

1. Something set before one for guidance or imitation.

2. A means of determining what a thing should be.

3. A fixed measure (Franklin Computer Dictionary, 2007 edition).

A good educational standard incorporates all three definitions. First, the standard is worthy of imitation and serves as a guide for planning appropriate curriculum. Secondly, it determines the learning objectives for a given grade level and subject area. Finally, it is specific and measurable. Educational content standards guide teaching and learning. They serve as the criteria for what should be learned at each grade level.

While the content standards determine the sequence of skills taught by the teacher, they do not guide the teacher in the development of the 21st century thinking process. The standards for the 21st century learner provide the teacher with the framework to introduce nonlinear thinking and problem solving. The 21st century standards are not content-specific. They can be applied to any subject discipline. It is important that the teacher instruct students both in the sequential, linear content standards and the 21st century nonlinear standards (AASL, 2007).

A good educational standard incorporates all three definitions. First, the standard is worthy of imitation and serves as a guide for planning appropriate curriculum. Secondly, it determines the learning objectives for a given grade level and subject area. Finally, it is specific and measurable.

The Sequential Content Standards

Why is it important to teach the sequential content standards? The answer is because the standards focus on the critical skills students need to know at each stage of content development. For example, the math standards focus on the critical mathematics operations and problem solving skills for each grade level.

Content standards are sequential. They provide skills that build upon each other. The mathematics standards in second grade require students to do repeated addition in multiplication. The third grade math standards build on the second grade multiplication standards and require students to multiply multi-digit numbers by one-digit numbers. Mastery of one grade level's math standards prepares students to master the next grade's standards.

If the goal for the students is to aim at mastering the standards, how does the teacher answer the question: *Why do we have to learn the standards?* The answer to this question is another question: *How can you hit a target if you don't know what the target is?* It is like wearing a blindfold and trying to hit a target with a bow and arrow. Standards focus the bow and arrow on the target. The blindfold is removed and students see exactly what they need to aim at. Once they know the target, students become amazing archers who are able to hit bulls'eyes.

The Best Practice teacher's role is to modify goals and adjust standards to students' readiness levels. Specific skills within each standard must be targeted. The assignments given to students must be realistic and capable of accomplishment. Standards-based activities must require effort but not be too difficult to make students give up trying.

Why is it important to teach the content standards? The answer is because the standards focus on the critical skills students need to know at each stage of content development.

Targeting Objectives

Standards are learned best when students focus on them daily. The teacher helps students to become familiar with the standards by posting them every day. The posted standards also help the teacher focus his or her own teaching on the standards. This may seem like a lot of work. Instead of doing this, the teacher might think *I'll just do what I want .....I'm sure my teaching will cover some standard*. The truth is this hit or miss approach does not cover any standard or skill adequately. The teacher's arrow has gone astray and is not even close to the bull's eye.

The teacher who targets the standards daily sets clear goals for students to follow. Students know what they are supposed to be learning even before instruction begins. When the goals of learning are well defined, extraneous data are easier to identify and eliminate and appropriate teaching strategies become more obvious. In addition to short term goals or learning objectives, students benefit from becoming aware of the "big picture." Long term goals put day-to-day activities in context. Goals help students set expectations for the week, the month and year.

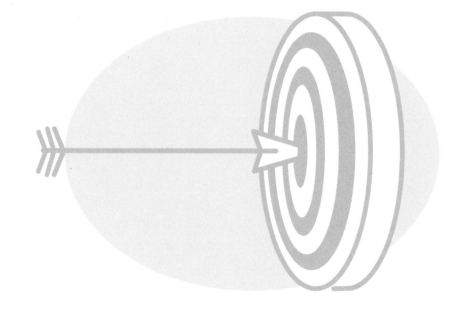

Working Backward with the Standards

One difficult task for the teacher instructing students in the grade-level content standards is to differentiate instruction for those students who have not mastered prerequisite standards or the standards from previous grade levels. Students cannot hit a target at the farthest distance until they learn to hit a closer target. The teacher, just like the archery coach," must identify and work backward through the standards to identify the gaps in students' learning. For example, students who do not know subject-verb agreement will have difficulty learning simple and compound sentences. Students who do not understand critical history subject area vocabulary will have difficulty reading core content history texts.

Working backward through the standards may be time consuming, but teaching students the prerequisite skills facilitates students' learning. Teachers who match readiness with appropriate instructional activities help students hit grade-level targets.

Bringing students up to grade level will most likely require additional time for practicing skills. It also requires the identification of the components of skills that students have not as yet mastered. Finally, it requires ongoing assessments (Content Standards for California Public Schools, 2000).

The focus on assessments is important. Each skill must be assessed to validate learning. Once one skill has been learned, students are ready to move to the next step. The focus is to build on what students have previously learned and to prepare students for future learning. Ultimately the goals of any lesson are understood in the context of their relation to grade-level content covered in earlier grades, and the content to be covered in later grades.

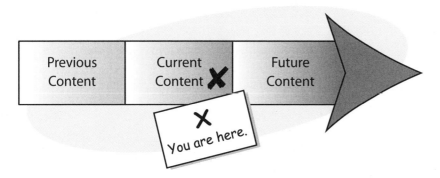

21st Century Learner Standards

Best Practice teachers, while focusing on the sequential content standards, also find time to address the interdisciplinary standards for the 21st century learner. Diagnostic, prescriptive teaching focuses on the content standards and at the same time develops students' critical and creative thinking power. The National Council of Teachers of Mathematics in their document on standards based teaching note:

The aim of prescriptive standards-based teaching is not just to instruct students in content skills. It is to teach students critical and creative thinking. Instructing students in the thinking process focuses on having students identify alternative solutions to problems rather than one right answer. When students find multiple solutions, they take cognitive leaps in learning (National Council of Teachers of Mathematics, 2007).

Although the focus of the National Council is on mathematics, the principle of identifying multiple solutions to problems crosses subject disciplines. The statement on standards based teaching challenges the one right answer model. Think of a traditional mathematics lesson on multiplication. In an assignment, the student who multiples two numbers using the "cake layer" method is marked correct, while the student who arrived at exactly the same answer using the algebraic FOIL rule is marked incorrect. Both students arrived at the correct answer but in different ways.

It is this very idea of addressing multiple ways to approach problem solving that is one of the premises on which the standards for the 21st century learner are based. These standards, created by the American Association of School Librarians target the thinking skills and the information literacy skills students need to function effectively across content areas. The standards are based on the premise that learners need skills and resources related to information literacy to:

1. Inquire, think critically, and gain knowledge.

2. Draw conclusions, make informed decisions, apply knowledge to new situations and create new knowledge.

> **Best Practice teachers, while focusing on the sequential content standards, also find time to address the interdisciplinary standards for the 21st century learner.**

3. Share knowledge and participate ethically and productively as members of our democratic society.

4. Pursue personal and aesthetic growth (AASL, 2007).

Each of the four overall standards addresses a critical element of 21st century learning. The first standard: *Inquire, think critically and gain knowledge* addresses the changing information environment in which students must learn to function. Multiple literacies, including digital, visual, textual and technological have been identified along with information literacy as essential skills. The exponential growth of information demands that all students acquire the thinking skills that will help them become independent learners. Students need to sift through the myriads of data to select, evaluate and use information appropriately and effectively (AASL, 2007).

As students learn the science content standard *Classify objects according to appropriate criteria*, they also need to apply the first 21st century inquiry standard. They first must formulate a testable strategic question. The use of inquiry is then required for students to answer their question. A viable answer is dependent on students' ability to think critically and evaluate the reliability and validity of data from both textual and digital sources.

The second 21st century standard is *Draw conclusions, make informed decisions, apply knowledge to new situations, and create new knowledge*. This standard continues the inquiry-based research process by applying the critical thinking skills (analysis, synthesis, evaluation and organization) as well as creative thinking skills. Students again must become proficient at adapting information strategies to each specific resource. They must also seek additional resources when clear conclusions cannot be drawn (AASL, 2007).

Think of the history standard: *List the reasons for the wave of immigration from Northern Europe to the United States and describe the growth in the number, size, and spatial arrangements of cities (e.g., Irish immigrants and the Great Irish Famine)*. As students research the reasons for immigration, they must evaluate sources on the World Wide Web.

It is through the evaluation process that students draw conclusions about why people in the past immigrated to the United States. They apply this knowledge to analyze the current reasons for immigration.

It is important as the teacher evaluates students' mastery of both the content history standard and the 21st century learner standard that he or she consider these in relation to the skills, dispositions, responsibilities and self assessment strategies that students need for learning.

Skills	Dispositions	Responsibilities	Self-Assessment
Key abilities for under-standing, thinking and learning	Beliefs and attitudes that guide thinking that can be measured through actions taken	Key behaviors for independent research, investigation and problem solving	Self reflection on learning

(AASL, 2007)

The critical questions that the teacher must ask are: *Do students have the skills to explore a topic of study in a group? Do learners have the critical thinking skills to evaluate their findings? Can students contribute and share their knowledge with their peers?*

These questions are addressed in the third 21st century standard: *Share knowledge and participate ethically and productively as members of our democratic society.*

This standard addresses team or cooperative learning as the preferred mode for the 21st century. Students benefit from learning from peers both in face-to-face situations and through technological applications. Global learners are students from around the world who connect with each other through technology. One of the goals for 21st century learners is to apply knowledge to address community and global issues.

The exponential growth of information demands that all students acquire the thinking skills that will help them become independent learners.

The third 21st century standard of sharing knowledge can also be addressed as students learn global languages for cross cultural communication. The foreign language standard *Students use the language both within and beyond the school setting* can be applied using technology. Students can communicate on a personal level with speakers of the languages they are learning through email, audio, blogs and videoconferencing.

The final 21st century learner standard is *Pursue personal and aesthetic growth*. This standard addresses the need for students to become self directed learners or pursue knowledge for personal growth. This is the self actualization stage of learning.

Students become self directed learners by applying the skills they learned in the content standards. These skills become the foundation of the thinking process. There are two functions of the content standards in relation to the thinking process. The first function is to impart the information in the standards themselves. The second function targets the information in the standards to carry out some thinking purpose: decision, action, choice, plan, design or pleasure. These dual functions of the thinking process contribute to the development and expansion of the mind.

All the content frameworks state: *The scholarly and scientific disciplines represent methods of study which have through millennia of sustained effort, for liberating the powers of the human mind* (California Science Content Standards, 2000). It is through the application of both the content standards and the 21st century standards that students become more than liberated; they become motivated to learn and prosper. A complete list of 21st Century Interdisciplinary Critical and Creative Thinking Problem Solving Standards can be found on pages 127-132.

In conclusion, it may be stated that education must now consider learning as a dual process involving both linear and nonlinear thinking. Students must not only be instructed in content standards, they must be taught how to apply the standards in a critical and creative way to solve the global challenges.

While this is the goal for 21st century education, recent nationwide polls revealed that the majority of Americans are deeply concerned that the United States' educational system is not keeping up with global changes. They are concerned that the schools are not keeping pace with the modern workforce. Americans realize that a 21st century education must incorporate a different set of skills that reflect the changing economic demands.

Businesses echo the public sentiment in stating that United States' students need an expanded set of thinking skills for their success in the globally interconnected society and workforce of the 21st century (The Partnership for 21st Century Skills, 2009). Business leaders state that 21st century skills must be integrated with subject area standards. These skills include problem solving, innovation and creativity.

The change necessary to transform education to the 21st century vision begins with the teacher in each classroom. Change is made one classroom at a time. It is through the efforts of individual teachers that students will become prepared for the 21st century world that exists now and extends into the future.

Think About Discussion Questions

1. Think about how you would integrate the 21st Century Learner Standards on pages 118-119 to teach one of your grade-level content standards.

2. Think about the difference between linear and nonlinear standards in relation to what you read in this chapter. Evaluate why both types of standards are important.

Reflection Upon the 21st Century Learner Standards

1. Reflect on the idea of creating independent learners that is addressed in the fourth *21st Century Learner Standard on page 119.* Evaluate how many students in your class are independent learners. Describe the results of your analysis and what you can do to get students to this level.

2. Create a standard that you think is important for the 21st century learner.

Chapter 7

Standards and Activities for the 21ST Century

Research shows that students remember the things they experience. They remember the things that have meaning and are real. Authentic experiences that have intrinsic value for students include: Questioning and Observing, Reasoning and Problem Solving and Communicating and Applying.

Now that you've learned the power of teaching students to develop their own strategic questions and problem solve both linearly and nonlinearly through the 21st century open-ended brainstorming model, you may want to create interdisciplinary projects which require students to link information. This will help students develop the powerful skill of *infolinking*. As you come up with problems that foster multiple solutions, you may want to introduce the 21st century learner standards in combination with the content standards. This section will give you a complete list of 21st Century Interdisciplinary Critical and Creative Thinking Problem Solving Standards as well as a number of problem solving activities to use with your students. These problem-solving activities can be done individually or in small groups. Remember that having students work in pairs or in small cooperative groups helps students communicate their ideas and consider these ideas from multiple perspectives. Students benefit from being able to test their ideas against those of a partner. How and when you use the activities in this section is up to you. As you watch students asking questions and problem solving by brainstorming with each other, you can feel satisfied that you are laying the foundation for students to be critical and creative thinkers who can research and integrate information in both textual and digital formats. Now let the powerful 21st century questioning and problem solving begin!

21st Century Interdisciplinary Critical and Creative Thinking and Problem Solving Standards

I. **Apply Higher Level Critical Thinking to Interdisciplinary Problem Solving.**

I.1 Use convergent thinking for problem solving. Use critical thinking to evaluate the evidence to form conclusions.

I.2 Analyze information using prior knowledge and new learning based on research.

I.3 Use critical thinking to formulate *Knowledge questions* as the basis for the formulating a Strategic question.

I.4 Formulate a *Strategic question* based on the answers to *Knowledge questions*. Answer the *Strategic question* through the problem solving process.

I.5 Evaluate interdisciplinary information found in text-based and digital sources on the basis of reliability and validity.

I.6 Make interdisciplinary inferences based on textual and digital information and apply these inferences to problem solving.

I.7 Use an inquiry process asking *Why questions* to evaluate, and select sources to answer questions during problem solving.

I.8 Analyze facts gathered from digital and textual sources to determine which are research-based facts and which are opinions.

I.9 Formulate a point of view based on the critical analysis of facts and concepts.

I.10 Identify and demonstrate mastery of the digital tools for accessing information.

I.11 Apply critical thinking to linear problem solving by posing *Strategic questions* and researching the answers by integrating interdisciplinary facts, concepts and principles.

I.12 Apply critical-thinking skills (analysis, synthesis, evaluation, organization) to construct new interdisciplinary understandings through problem solving.

I.13 Apply rules of writing and grammar to integrate interdisciplinary knowledge in a written summary.

I.14 Demonstrate interdisciplinary research skills by selecting resources for problem solving that have validity and reliability.

I.15 Use critical thinking to judge the importance of the researched facts to the solution of an interdisciplinary problem.

I.16 Adapt problem solving by continuing to analyze information. If A is true then B is_____?

I.17 Conduct multidisciplinary problem solving to address current world issues.

I.18 Construct interdisciplinary understandings through examining, discussing and working on challenging problems with competing points of view.

I.19 Demonstrate a critical understanding of copyright/ intellectual property rights.

I.20 Apply critical thinking questions and problem solving to the core curriculum.

I.21 Follow ethical and legal guidelines in gathering and using information for interdisciplinary problem solving.

I.22 Use a multimodality approach to interdisciplinary problem solving.

1.23 Demonstrate mastery of media applications to interdisciplinary problem solving.

I.24 Demonstrate the ability to move from linear to nonlinear interdisciplinary problem solving.

I.25 Use a continuous improvement model to evaluate the results of problem solving.

I.26 Demonstrate the strategic use of feedback from teachers and peers to formulate new *Strategic research questions* for continued problem solving.

I.27 Apply critical interdisciplinary problem solving to global issues.

I.28 Implement global languages for critical problem solving.

II. Think Creatively: Transform and Create New Interdisciplinary Knowledge

II.1 Demonstrate generative creative thinking and problem solving that moves from what is to what is possible.

II.2 Apply divergent thinking to interdisciplinary problem solving.

II.3 Demonstrate the use of interdisciplinary nonlinear problem solving to formulate Strategic questions that lead to the asking of new questions.

II.4 Demonstrate the use of technology and other information tools to synthesize facts and concepts for creative interdisciplinary problem solving.

II.5 Formulate and apply *What if?* questions to transform knowledge and create new understandings.

II.6 Demonstrate the ability to use multimedia applications to create products that manifest original ideas.

II.7 Synthesize facts and concepts and apply knowledge to interdisciplinary global challenges.

II.8 Demonstrate creative flexibility by integrating data from digital and textual resources to solve interdisciplinary problems.

II.9 Demonstrate associative creative questioning in problem solving. *How can I develop a new way to connect these steps or data to develop the idea of_____?*

II.10 Change a new product or idea through combining, substituting, eliminating, minimizing or reordering its elements through the interdisciplinary problem solving process.

II.11 Demonstrate personal productivity by inventing applications for learning.

II.12 Understand how to use novelty to create something new through interdisciplinary problem solving.

II.13 Demonstrate the use of lateral thinking and creative problem solving to create a multitude of possibilities to transform knowledge.

II.14 Integrate diverse and global perspectives in multidisciplinary creative problem solving.

II.15 Create interdisciplinary solutions through *Design* (Pink, 2006).

II.16 Demonstrate the use of narrative imagining in problem solving by using *Story* (Pink, 2006).

II.17 Apply global languages and *Lingolinking* to creative problem solving.

II.18 Apply intuition to the creative problem solving process.

II.19 Demonstrate the use of applied imagination to creatively solve global challenges.

II.20 Use a multidimensional approach to creative thinking and problem solving.

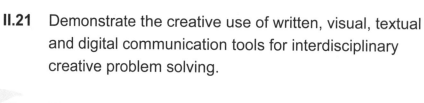

II.21 Demonstrate the creative use of written, visual, textual and digital communication tools for interdisciplinary creative problem solving.

III. Work in Self Directed Teams

III.1 Engage in critical and creative problem solving with a team of learners. Share new understandings and new applications of knowledge.

III.2 Share ideas and collaborate with diverse team members to integrate multicultural understandings and approaches to problem solving.

III.3 Serve as the *Team Leader*. Assign roles to students such as researcher, illustrator, to facilitate the process of interdisciplinary problem solving.

III.4 Integrate technology and other information tools in cooperative group problem solving. Present group solutions through multimodality presentations.

III.5 Brainstorm the solutions to classroom, school, community and global issues and challenges in cooperative heterogeneous groups.

III.6 Demonstrate the use of consensus-building in *Self-Directed Work Teams.*

III.7 Apply critical and creative problem solving strategies by working with peers in cooperative heterogeneous and homogeneous groups.

III.8 Demonstrate leadership and adaptability by presenting and integrating the viewpoints and expertise of others for interdisciplinary problem solving.

III.9 Participate actively with others in discussions by asking critical and creative questions.

III.10 Demonstrate teamwork by working productively with others.

III.11 Demonstrate effective use of rubrics for group self assessment.

III.12 Apply interdisciplinary critical and creative cooperative group problem solving by seeking diverse multilingual, community and global perspectives.

III.13 Demonstrate the ability to become a team player by accepting and honoring the culture, language and perspective of other team members.

III.14 Participate in a number of interdisciplinary group problem solving activities to transform knowledge using applications of *Design, Story and Visual Communication* (Pink, 2006).

III.15 Create products in cooperative groups that can be applied to address authentic community and global challenges.

III.16 Participate and exchange ideas with peers in discussions related to interdisciplinary core curriculum and social issues in the community.

III.17 Demonstrate the appropriate use of information in the form of a debate on interdisciplinary issues.

III.18 Apply multiple solutions to creative problem solving in *Self-directed Work Teams.*

III.19 Demonstrate the application of democratic principles in group problem solving.

III.20 Participate in group assessments of learning and devise more effective team-building strategies for creative problem solving.

III.21 Participate in group assessments to evaluate the quality and effectiveness of the applied research or the product.

III.22 Demonstrate the ability to take on diverse roles in a group setting.

III.23 Apply 21st century communication skills for interdisciplinary group problem solving.

IV. **Participate in Community-based Interdisciplinary Learning**

IV.1 Demonstrate the use of the *Case Study Service Model* which incorporates inquiry with community service.

IV.2 Make connections and applications of school learning to community and global problem solving.

IV.3 Engage in public debates in various digital formats on issues related to the community.

IV.4 Demonstrate the ability to frame community issues in a persuasive essay.

IV.5 Connect community issues to personal interests and previous knowledge and experience.

IV.6 Explore career options and their impact on the welfare of community members.

IV.7 Utilize social and cultural networks as information tools to gather and share interdisciplinary knowledge.

IV.8 Demonstrate initiative in creating digital forums for the dissemination of knowledge.

IV.9 Apply information from the past to create resources for the community of the future.

IV.10 Apply knowledge to find appropriate solutions to community and personal challenges.

IV.11 Demonstrate motivation by seeking information to answer critical questions relating to community and global issues that go beyond the classroom.

IV.12 Demonstrate the ability to evaluate and synthesize new ideas by considering divergent community or global perspectives.

IV.13 Utilize a variety of technological resources to find appropriate interdisciplinary information in problem solving that takes into account multicultural perspectives.

IV.14 Develop an appreciation of global languages and their accompanying cultural perspectives.

IV.15 Participate in the academic exchange of ideas, both electronically and in person.

IV.17 Recognize the various communities that contribute to learning.

IV.18 Read, view and listen to information gathered from diverse community and global sources.

IV.19 Collaborate with educational peers, family and community members. Synthesize perspectives for creative interdisciplinary problem solving.

V. **Apply Continuous Improvement Strategies**

V.1 Evaluate individual strengths and weaknesses.

V.2 Implement the philosophy of learning as a nonlinear continuous process of becoming.

V.3 Demonstrate confidence and self-direction in learning and acquiring interdisciplinary knowledge using textual, multimedia and digital sources.

V.4 Synthesize and evaluate new information based on cultural and social context.

V.6 Implement ideas gained from curriculum with intuition to transform knowledge into new personal understandings.

V.7 Evaluate how learned information can be applied to career and personal goals. (Ventriglia, 2009)

Problem Solving Activities

These are samples of problem solving activities that can be used with interdisciplinary learning.

Flour Bags

A deliveryman from the Dusty White Flour Mill has been packing his truck for the morning deliveries. One of his stops is at the Flaky Crust Bakery where they want exactly 100 pounds of flour for the holiday baking. The Dusty White Flour Mill only packs in bags of 16, 17, 23, or 24 pounds each. Can the deliveryman deliver this 100 pound order with these 4 different bag sizes? If not, how close can he come to making up the 100 pounds?

Coin Math

At the game arcade the change machine takes only quarters. For each quarter that is put in, it gives out different combinations of change. The machine can only give up to fifteen coins at a time. How many combinations can you make on the chart below?

Coin	Example	1st Try	2nd Try	3rd Try	4th Try	5th Try	6th Try	7th Try	8th Try	9th Try
1 Cent	5									
5 Cents	2									
10 Cents	1									
Total	25 cents									

Horseshoe Pitching

In the game of horseshoes, a person can score either a ringer for six points, a leaner for three points, and closest to the stake for two points. If a person only scores ringers or leaners but does not get any points for closest to the stake, what scores cannot be achieved if the person scored under 30 points?

Spotted Ladybugs

Ladybugs, some with six spots and some with four spots, were sharing a leaf. The total number of spots was 42.
How many four spotted and six spotted ladybugs were there?

Cube Structure

For this activity you will need five cubes: 2 yellow, 1 red, 1 green, and 1 blue.

Directions for a single student:
Read and follow the written directions below to build the described structure.

1. The red cube shares one face each with a yellow cube and green cube, and one edge with the other yellow cube.
2. The green cube shares a face with the red cube and one face with a yellow cube, and an edge with the other yellow cube.
3. The yellow cubes share a vertex with each other.
4. The blue cube shares one face with the green cube, and one edge with a yellow cube.

Directions for paired activity:

1. Set up a screen between you and your partner.
2. Both students have blocks. One student constructs a block structure.
3. This student now describes their structure using terminology as in the above activity.
4. The student on the other side follows the oral directions, trying to duplicate the block structure.

Four Coin Puzzles

Four coins in a row total 75 cents. The first coin is ten times the value of the last coin. What are the coins? What is their order in the row?

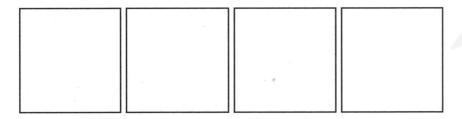

Two rows of two coins each, forming a square, total 50 cents. The largest coin is in the top left hand corner.
In the bottom row, the first coin is twice the value of the second coin. What are the coins? Where are they in the square?

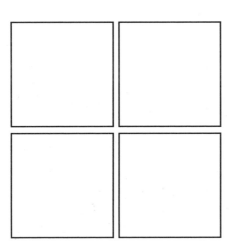

Pentominoes

1. There is only one way to arrange two squares.
   (at least one of the edges of each square must match up with the edge of another square.)

2. There are only two ways to arrange three squares. If you can make one arrangement look like another by flipping or turning it, then it is not a new arrangement.

3. There are only five ways to arrange four squares.

4. How many ways can you arrange five squares?

21st Century Questioning and Problem Solving: Infolinking

A Little Logic

1. Three puzzle pieces (a triangle, a square, and a circle) with holes in them are stacked on a rod.

2. Each piece has a hole of a shape different from itself.

3. These three facts are true of the stack:
   The triangular piece is above the piece with the round hole.
   The square hole is above the triangular hole.
   The circular piece is on the bottom of the stack.

   What shape is in the middle of the stack?

   Where in the stack is the triangular hole?

Choose the Operation

Read each question.
Check the operation needed to solve the problem.
Write a number sentence.

Problem	+	-	x	÷	Number Sentence
1. Maxie is building 5 tricycles with Legos. How many wheels will she need?					
2. Bill shares a dozen cookies with three friends. How many cookies will they each have?					
3. For the pet show, 3 children brought their cats, 5 brought their dogs, and 4 brought birds. How many legs do they all have?					

Just the Facts

Solve each word problem.

Draw a line through the information you didn't need to use to solve the problem.

1. Jill had 50 cents to spend. Three dimes and four nickels jingled in her pocket as she ran to the store. When she arrived, she discovered she had lost two of the coins. What could be the greatest amount of money she could spend?

2. Fred overslept and awoke at 9:25 a.m. The 8:45 a.m. school bus left without him. After a quick breakfast, he left for school at 10:05 a.m. How long did it take him to get ready for school?

3. In five days' time, Mary had read 8 library books. She was allowed to check out up to 3 books at a time. If she continued reading at this rate for another ten days, how many books will she have read altogether?

4. The board was now 3 1/4 feet long. Jay had cut it 6 inches too short for the shelf. The piece left from the original board was only 2 1/2 feet long. What was the length of the original board before Jay began sawing?

5. George folded half of his newspapers for his paper route in 20 minutes and 35 seconds. He is able to fold four papers in about 1 1/2 minutes. If it took him 10 seconds longer to fold the other half of the papers, how much time did it take to fold all the papers?

Target Practice

Herman threw three darts at the target.

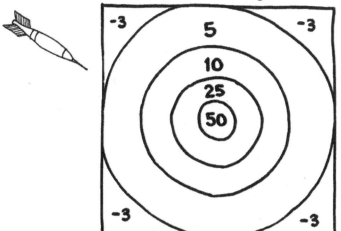

He scored 32 points.

Draw the darts on the target to show the areas he hit.

Square Fractions

If  = 1

Then  = 1/4   and [ ] = 1/16

What does [ ] equal? _____

Please explain your answer.

Use words and drawings.

Determining Area

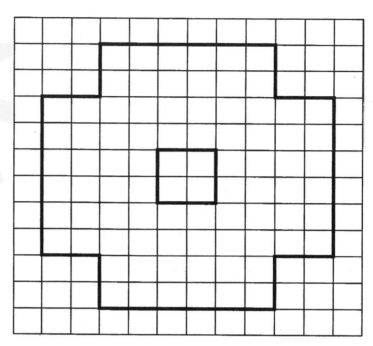

What is the area of this shape?

Area = _____ square units.

Explain how you found the answer.

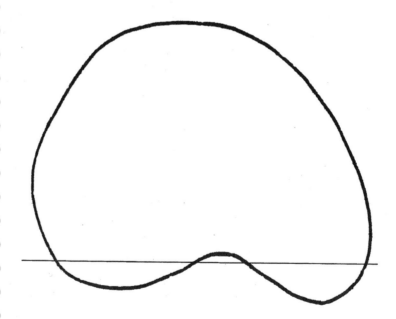

What is the area of this shape?

Area = _____ square units.

Explain how you found the answer.

Predictions

If you spin the paperclip 40 times, how many times will it land on the number one?

- Make a prediction. _____

- Spin the paperclip 40 times and tally the results on the chart below.

1	2	3

- Explain your prediction and the results.
  (Use words and drawings.)

To use the spinner, put a pencil point through a paperclip and hold them on the center of the circle.

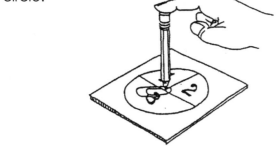

With the other hand, flick the paperclip to spin it around the pencil point.

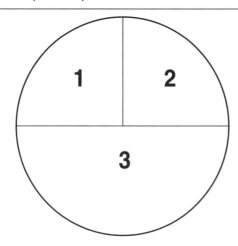

Marbles, Worms, and Pennies
(Estimation Activities)

It took 45 handfuls of marbles to fill this jar. About how many marbles are in the jar?

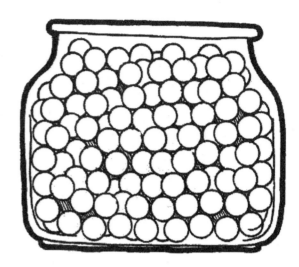

About how many inches long is this earthworm?

How can you estimate the length without measuring it?

Science Fact: Worms can vary in length from 1/25 inch to 11 feet.

About how many pennies would it take to make a stack two inches high?

Math Journaling Prompts

Students use a math journal to respond to mathematical prompts. The mathematical prompts are given to the students verbally and in writing on the board or overhead. These are examples of mathematical prompts:

1. Write these mathematical vocabulary terms and your own definitions: pentagon, obtuse, angle, scalene, protractor etc.

2. Write the mathematical rule for_____.
    Read and explain the rule to a partner.

3. There are several ways to solve this problem.
    Which method is your favorite? Why is it your favorite?
    Read your explanation to a partner.

4. Write an explanation about what you learned in mathematics today. Use diagrams or charts for your explanation. Read your explanation to a partner.

5. Write what you know about (multiplication, division, algebra etc.) Tell what you know to a partner.

6. Find something that you learned today that is similar to something you already know. Use a Venn diagram to show similarities.

7. These are the questions I have about what I learned today in mathematics.

8. Write a possible problem for this unit. Have a partner solve it.

9. Explain how you used math this week outside of Math class. Write the further questions you have.

10. My three goals for this unit are...

11. Is math your favorite subject? Why or why not?

12. Write an explanation for a classmate who was absent for today's lesson.

13. Choose one of last week's journal entries and revise it. Either rewrite it so it becomes clearer or draw a picture to go along with your explanation.

14. Write an explanation for how you and your partners were able or not able to solve the problem of the week. (Teach support web site: http://mathforum.org/library/resource_types/pow_pom)

Mathematical Reasoning Standards

Focus Standards for Problem Solving in K-12 Classrooms

Kinder

Statistics, Data Analysis, and Probability

1.0 Students collect information about objects and events in their environment:

1.1 Pose information questions; collect data; and record the results using objects, pictures, and picture graphs.

1.2 Identify, describe, and extend simple patterns (such as circles or triangles) by referring to their shapes, sizes, or colors.

Mathematical Reasoning and Problem Solving

1.0 Students make decisions about how to set up a problem:

1.1 Determine the approach, materials, and strategies to be used.

1.2 Use tools and strategies, such as manipulatives or sketches, to model problems.

2.0 Students solve problems in reasonable ways and justify their reasoning:

2.1 Explain the reasoning used with concrete objects and/ or pictorial representations.

2.2 Make precise calculations and check the validity of the results in the context of the problem.

1st Grade

Statistics, Data Analysis, and Probability

1.0 Students organize, represent, and compare data by category on simple graphs and charts:

1.1 Sort objects and data by common attributes and describe the categories.

1.2 Represent and compare data (e.g., largest, smallest, most often, least often) by using pictures, bar graphs, tally charts, and picture graphs.

2.0 Students sort objects and create and describe patterns by numbers, shapes, sizes, rhythms, or colors:

2.1 Describe, extend, and explain ways to get to a next element in simple repeating patterns (e.g., rhythmic, numeric, color, and shape).

Mathematical Reasoning and Problem Solving

1.0 Students make decisions about how to set up a problem:

1.1 Determine the approach, materials, and strategies to be used.

1.2 Use tools, such as manipulatives or sketches, to model problems.

2.0 Students solve problems and justify their reasoning:

2.1 Explain the reasoning used and justify the procedures selected.

2.2 Make precise calculations and check the validity of the results from the context of the problem.

3.0 Students note connections between one problem and another.

2nd Grade

Statistics, Data Analysis, and Probability

1.0 Students collect numerical data and record, organize, display, and interpret the data on bar graphs and other representations:

1.1 Record numerical data in systematic ways, keeping track of what has been counted.

1.2 Represent the same data set in more than one way (e.g., bar graphs and charts with tallies).

1.3 Identify features of data sets (range and mode).

1.4 Ask and answer simple questions related to data representations.

2.0 Students demonstrate an understanding of patterns and how patterns grow and describe them in general ways:

2.1 Recognize, describe, and extend patterns and determine a next term in linear patterns (e.g., 4, 8, 12 ...; the number of ears on one horse, two horses, three horses, four horses).

2.2 Solve problems involving simple number patterns.

Mathematical Reasoning and Problem Solving

1.0 Students make decisions about how to set up a problem:

1.1 Determine the approach, materials, and strategies to be used.

1.2 Use tools, such as manipulatives or sketches, to model problems.

2.0 Students solve problems and justify their reasoning:

2.1 Defend the reasoning used and justify the procedures selected.

2.2 Make precise calculations and check the validity of the results in the context of the problem.

3.0 Students note connections between one problem and another.

3rd Grade

Statistics, Data Analysis, and Probability

1.0 Students conduct simple probability experiments by determining the number of possible outcomes and make simple predictions:

1.1 Identify whether common events are certain, likely, unlikely, or improbable.

1.2 Record the possible outcomes for a simple event (e.g., tossing a coin) and systematically keep track of the outcomes when the event is repeated many times.

1.3 Summarize and display the results of probability experiments in a clear and organized way (e.g., use a bar graph or a line plot).

1.4 Use the results of probability experiments to predict future events (e.g., use a line plot to predict the temperature forecast for the next day).

Mathematical Reasoning and Problem Solving

1.0 Students make decisions about how to approach problems:

1.1 Analyze problems by identifying relationships, distinguishing relevant from irrelevant information, sequencing and prioritizing information, and observing patterns.

1.2 Determine when and how to break a problem into simpler parts.

2.0 Students use strategies, skills, and concepts in finding solutions:

2.1 Use estimation to verify the reasonableness of calculated results.

2.2 Apply strategies and results from simpler problems to more complex problems.

2.3 Use a variety of methods, such as words, numbers, symbols, charts, graphs, tables, diagrams, and models, to explain mathematical reasoning.

2.4 Express the solution clearly and logically by using the appropriate mathematical notation and terms and clear language; support solutions with evidence in both verbal and symbolic work.

2.5 Indicate the relative advantages of exact and approximate solutions to problems and give answers to a specified degree of accuracy.

2.6 Make precise calculations and check the validity of the results from the context of the problem.

3.0 Students move beyond a particular problem by generalizing to other situations:

3.1 Evaluate the reasonableness of the solution in the context of the original situation.

3.2 Note the method of deriving the solution and demonstrate a conceptual understanding of the derivation by solving similar problems.

3.3 Develop generalizations of the results obtained and apply them in other circumstances.

4th Grade

Statistics, Data Analysis, and Probability

1.0 Students organize, represent, and interpret numerical and categorical data and clearly communicate their findings:

1.1 Formulate survey questions; systematically collect and represent data on a number line; and coordinate graphs, tables, and charts.

1.2 Identify the mode(s) for sets of categorical data and the mode(s), median, and any apparent outliers for numerical data sets.

1.3 Interpret one-and two-variable data graphs to answer questions about a situation.

2.0 Students make predictions for simple probability situations:

2.1 Represent all possible outcomes for a simple probability situation in an organized way (e.g., tables, grids, tree diagrams).

2.2 Express outcomes of experimental probability situations verbally and numerically (e.g., 3 out of 4; 3 /4).

Mathematical Reasoning and Problem Solving

1.0 Students make decisions about how to approach problems:

1.1 Analyze problems by identifying relationships, distinguishing relevant from irrelevant information, sequencing and prioritizing information, and observing patterns.

1.2 Determine when and how to break a problem into simpler parts.

2.0 Students use strategies, skills, and concepts in finding solutions:

2.1 Use estimation to verify the reasonableness of calculated results.

2.2 Apply strategies and results from simpler problems to more complex problems.

2.3 Use a variety of methods, such as words, numbers, symbols, charts, graphs, tables, diagrams, and models, to explain mathematical reasoning.

2.4 Express the solution clearly and logically by using the appropriate mathematical notation and terms and clear language; support solutions with evidence in both verbal and symbolic work.

2.5 Indicate the relative advantages of exact and approximate solutions to problems and give answers to a specified degree of accuracy.

2.6 Make precise calculations and check the validity of the results from the context of the problem.

3.0 Students move beyond a particular problem by generalizing to other situations:

3.1 Evaluate the reasonableness of the solution in the context of the original situation.

3.2 Note the method of deriving the solution and demonstrate a conceptual understanding of the derivation by solving similar problems.

3.3 Develop generalizations of the results obtained and apply them in other circumstances.

5th Grade

Statistics, Data Analysis, and Probability

1.0 Students display, analyze, compare, and interpret different data sets, including data sets of different sizes:

1.1 Know the concepts of mean, median, and mode; compute and compare simple examples to show that they may differ.

1.2 Organize and display single-variable data in appropriate graphs and representations (e.g., histogram, circle graphs) and explain which types of graphs are appropriate for various data sets.

1.3 Use fractions and percentages to compare data sets of different sizes.

1.4 Identify ordered pairs of data from a graph and interpret the meaning of the data in terms of the situation depicted by the graph.

1.5 Know how to write ordered pairs correctly; for example, (x, y).

Mathematical Reasoning and Problem Solving

1.0 Students make decisions about how to approach problems:

1.1 Analyze problems by identifying relationships, distinguishing relevant from irrelevant information, sequencing and prioritizing information, and observing patterns.

1.2 Determine when and how to break a problem into simpler parts.

2.0 Students use strategies, skills, and concepts in finding solutions:

2.1 Use estimation to verify the reasonableness of calculated results.

2.2 Apply strategies and results from simpler problems to more complex problems.

2.3 Use a variety of methods, such as words, numbers, symbols, charts, graphs, tables, diagrams, and models, to explain mathematical reasoning.

2.4 Express the solution clearly and logically by using the appropriate mathematical notation and terms and clear language; support solutions with evidence in both verbal and symbolic work.

2.5 Indicate the relative advantages of exact and approximate solutions to problems and give answers to a specified degree of accuracy.

2.6 Make precise calculations and check the validity of the results from the context of the problem.

3.0 Students move beyond a particular problem by generalizing to other situations:

3.1 Evaluate the reasonableness of the solution in the context of the original situation.

3.2 Note the method of deriving the solution and demonstrate a conceptual understanding of the derivation by solving similar problems.

3.3 Develop generalizations of the results obtained and apply them in other circumstances.

6th Grade

Statistics, Data Analysis, and Probability

1.0 Students compute and analyze statistical measurements for data sets:

1.1 Compute the range, mean, median, and mode of data sets.

1.2 Understand how additional data added to data sets may affect these computations of measures of central tendency.

1.3 Understand how the inclusion or exclusion of outliers affects measures of central tendency.

1.4 Know why a specific measure of central tendency (mean, median) provides the most useful information in a given context.

2.0 Students use data samples of a population and describe the characteristics and limitations of the samples:

2.1 Compare different samples of a population with the data from the entire population and identify a situation in which it makes sense to use a sample.

2.2 Identify different ways of selecting a sample (e.g., convenience sampling, responses to a survey, random sampling) and which method makes a sample more representative for a population.

2.3 Analyze data displays and explain why the way in which the question was asked might have influenced the results obtained and why the way in which the results were displayed might have influenced the conclusions reached.

2.4 Identify data that represent sampling errors and explain why the sample (and the display) might be biased.

2.5 Identify claims based on statistical data and, in simple cases, evaluate the validity of the claims.

3.0 Students determine theoretical and experimental probabilities and use these to make predictions about events:

3.1 Represent all possible outcomes for compound events in an organized way (e.g., tables, grids, tree diagrams) and express the theoretical probability of each outcome.

3.2 Use data to estimate the probability of future events (e.g., batting averages or number of accidents per mile driven).

3.3 Represent probabilities as ratios, proportions, decimals between 0 and 1, and percentages between 0 and 100 and verify that the probabilities computed are reasonable; know that if P is the probability of an event, $1-P$ is the probability of an event not occurring.

3.4 Understand that the probability of either of two disjoint events occurring is the sum of the two individual probabilities and that the probability of one event following another, in independent trials, is the product of the two probabilities.

3.5 Understand the difference between independent and dependent events.

Mathematical Reasoning and Problem Solving

1.0 Students make decisions about how to approach problems:

1.1 Analyze problems by identifying relationships, distinguishing relevant from irrelevant information, identifying missing information, sequencing and prioritizing information, and observing patterns.

1.2 Formulate and justify mathematical conjectures based on a general description of the mathematical question or problem posed.

1.3 Determine when and how to break a problem into simpler parts.

2.0 Students use strategies, skills, and concepts in finding solutions:

2.1   Use estimation to verify the reasonableness of calculated results.

2.2   Apply strategies and results from simpler problems to more complex problems.

2.3   Estimate unknown quantities graphically and solve problems by using logical reasoning and arithmetic and algebraic techniques.

2.4   Use a variety of methods, such as words, numbers, symbols, charts, graphs, tables, diagrams, and models, to explain mathematical reasoning.

2.5   Express the solution clearly and logically by using the appropriate mathematical notation and terms and clear language; support solutions with evidence in both verbal and symbolic work.

2.6   Indicate the relative advantages of exact and approximate solutions to problems and give answers to a specified degree of accuracy.

2.7   Make precise calculations and check the validity of the results from the context of the problem.

3.0 Students move beyond a particular problem by generalizing to other situations:

3.1   Evaluate the reasonableness of the solution in the context of the original situation.

3.2   Note the method of deriving the solution and demonstrate a conceptual understanding of the derivation by solving similar problems.

3.3   Develop generalizations of the results obtained and the strategies used and apply them in new problem situations.

7th Grade

Statistics, Data Analysis, and Probability

1.0 **Students collect, organize, and represent data sets that have one or more variables and identify relationships among variables within a data set by hand and through the use of an electronic spreadsheet software program:**

    1.1   Know various forms of display for data sets, including a stem-and-leaf plot or box-and-whisker plot; use the forms to display a single set of data or to compare two sets of data.

    1.2   Represent two numerical variables on a scatter plot and informally describe how the data points are distributed and any apparent relationship that exists between the two variables (e.g., between time spent on homework and grade level).

    1.3   Understand the meaning of, and be able to compute, the minimum, the lower quartile, the median, the upper quartile, and the maximum of a data set.

Mathematical Reasoning and Problem Solving

1.0 **Students make decisions about how to approach problems:**

    1.1   Analyze problems by identifying relationships, distinguishing relevant from irrelevant information, identifying missing information, sequencing and prioritizing information, and observing patterns.

    1.2   Formulate and justify mathematical conjectures based on a general description of the mathematical question or problem posed.

    1.3   Determine when and how to break a problem into simpler parts.

2.0 Students use strategies, skills, and concepts in finding solutions:

2.1 Use estimation to verify the reasonableness of calculated results.

2.2 Apply strategies and results from simpler problems to more complex problems.

2.3 Estimate unknown quantities graphically and solve for them by using logical reasoning and arithmetic and algebraic techniques.

2.4 Make and test conjectures by using both inductive and deductive reasoning.

2.5 Use a variety of methods, such as words, numbers, symbols, charts, graphs, tables, diagrams, and models, to explain mathematical reasoning.

2.6 Express the solution clearly and logically by using the appropriate mathematical notation and terms and clear language; support solutions with evidence in both verbal and symbolic work.

2.7 Indicate the relative advantages of exact and approximate solutions to problems and give answers to a specified degree of accuracy.

2.8 Make precise calculations and check the validity of the results from the context of the problem.

3.0 Students determine a solution is complete and move beyond a particular problem by generalizing to other situations:

3.1 Evaluate the reasonableness of the solution in the context of the original situation.

3.2 Note the method of deriving the solution and demonstrate a conceptual understanding of the derivation by solving similar problems.

3.3 Develop generalizations of the results obtained and the strategies used and apply them to new problem situations.

8th – 12th Grade

Algebra 1

Symbolic reasoning and calculations with symbols are central in algebra. Through the study of algebra, a student develops an understanding of the symbolic language of mathematics and the sciences. In addition, algebraic skills and concepts are developed and used in a wide variety of problem-solving situations.

5.0 **Students solve multistep problems, including word problems, involving linear equations and linear inequalities in one variable and provide justification for each step.**

6.0 **Students graph a linear equation and compute the x- and y- intercepts (e.g., graph $2x + 6y = 4$). They are also able to sketch the region defined by linear inequality (e.g., they sketch the region defined by $2x + 6y < 4$).**

15.0 **Students apply algebraic techniques to solve rate problems, work problems, and percent mixture problems.**

18.0 **Students determine whether a relation defined by a graph, a set of ordered pairs, or a symbolic expression is a function and justify the conclusion.**

24.0 **Students use and know simple aspects of a logical argument:**

    24.1 Students explain the difference between inductive and deductive reasoning and identify and provide examples of each.

    24.2 Students identify the hypothesis and conclusion in logical deduction.

    24.3 Students use counterexamples to show that an assertion is false and recognize that a single counterexample is sufficient to refute an assertion.

25.0 Students use properties of the number system to judge the validity of results, to justify each step of a procedure, and to prove or disprove statements:

25.1 Students use properties of numbers to construct simple, valid arguments (direct and indirect) for, or formulate counterexamples to, claimed assertions.

25.2 Students judge the validity of an argument according to whether the properties of the real number system and the order of operations have been applied correctly at each step.

25.3 Given a specific algebraic statement involving linear, quadratic, or absolute value expressions or equations or inequalities, students determine whether the statement is true sometimes, always, or never.

Geometry

The geometry skills and concepts developed in this discipline are useful to all students. Aside from learning these skills and concepts, students will develop their ability to construct formal, logical arguments and proofs in geometric settings and problems.

1.0 Students demonstrate understanding by identifying and giving examples of undefined terms, axioms, theorems, and inductive and deductive reasoning.

2.0 Students write geometric proofs, including proofs by contradiction.

3.0 Students construct and judge the validity of a logical argument and give counterexamples to disprove a statement.

4.0 Students prove basic theorems involving congruence and similarity.

5.0 Students prove that triangles are congruent or similar, and they are able to use the concept of corresponding parts of congruent triangles.

14.0 Students prove the Pythagorean theorem.

15.0 Students use the Pythagorean theorem to determine distance and find missing lengths of sides of right triangles.

17.0 Students prove theorems by using coordinate geometry, including the midpoint of a line segment, the distance formula, and various forms of equations of lines and circles.

Algebra 2

This discipline complements and expands the mathematical content and concepts of algebra I and geometry. Students who master algebra II will gain experience with algebraic solutions of problems in various content areas, including the solution of systems of quadratic equations, logarithmic and exponential functions, the binomial theorem, and the complex number system.

8.0 Students solve and graph quadratic equations by factoring, completing the square, or using the quadratic formula. Students apply these techniques in solving word problems. They also solve quadratic equations in the complex number system.

11.0 Students prove simple laws of logarithms.

11.1 Students understand the inverse relationship between exponents and logarithms and use this relationship to solve problems involving logarithms and exponents.

11.2 Students judge the validity of an argument according to whether the properties of real numbers, exponents, and logarithms have been applied correctly at each step.

15.0 Students determine whether a specific algebraic statement involving rational expressions, radical expressions, or logarithmic or exponential functions is sometimes true, always true, or never true.

19.0 Students use combinations and permutations to compute probabilities.

21.0 Students apply the method of mathematical induction to prove general statements about the positive integers.

25.0 Students use properties from number systems to justify steps in combining and simplifying functions.

Trigonometry

Trigonometry uses the techniques that students have previously learned from the study of algebra and geometry. The trigonometric functions studied are defined geometrically rather than in terms of algebraic equations. Facility with these functions as well as the ability to prove basic identities regarding them is especially important for students intending to study calculus, more advanced mathematics, physics and other sciences, and engineering in college.

3.0 Students know the identity $\cos^2(x) + \sin^2(x) = 1$:

    3.1 Students prove that this identity is equivalent to the Pythagorean theorem (i.e., students can prove this identity by using the Pythagorean theorem and, conversely, they can prove the Pythagorean theorem as a consequence of this identity).

    3.2 Students prove other trigonometric identities and simplify others by using the identity $\cos^2(x) + \sin^2(x) = 1$. For example, students use this identity to prove that $\sec^2(x) = \tan^2(x) + 1$.

12.0 Students use trigonometry to determine unknown sides or angles in right triangles.

13.0 Students know the law of sines and the law of cosines and apply those laws to solve problems.

14.0 Students determine the area of a triangle, given one angle and the two adjacent sides.

Bibliography

Abey, N. (2005). Developing 21st century teaching and learning: Dialogic literacy. *New Horizons for Learning* http://www.new horizons.org.

Alfke, D. (1974). Asking operational questions. *Science and Children*, 11, 17, 18-19.

American Association of School Librarians AASL. (2007). *21st Century learner standards.* Chicago, Illinois: American Library Association.

Anderson, H. O. Teaching for the future.(1999). *The Science Teacher*, 66, 8.

Anderson, T. H. and Armbruster, B.B. (1984). Content area textbooks. In. R.C. Anderson, J. Osborn and R.J. Tierney (Eds.) *Learning to read in American Schools: Basal readers and content texts.* Hillsdale, New York: Erlbaum.

Baumann, J. (1986). Effects of rewritten content text passages on middle school students' comprehension of main ideas: Making the inconsiderate considerate. *Journal of Reading Behavior*, 18, 1-22.

Beck I and McKeown, M. (2004). Transforming knowledge into professional resources: Six teachers implement a model of teaching and understanding text. *The Elementary School Journal*, 104, 5.

Beck, I. and McKeown, M. (2002). Questioning the author: Making sense of social studies. *Educational Leadership*, November.

Beck, I. and McKeown, M. (2001). Inviting students into the pursuit of meaning. *Educational Psychology Review*, 13, 3.

Beck, I. and McKeown and Sandora,C and Kucan, L. (1996). Questioning the author: A year long classroom implementation to engage students with text. *The Elementary School Journal*, 96, 4.

Beck, I. and McKeown and Gromoll, E. (1989). Learning from social studies texts. Cognition and Instruction, 6, 2, 99-158.

Berghoff, B.and Egawa, K. (2001). No more 'rocks': Grouping to give students control of their learning. *The Reading Teacher*, Volume 44, Number 8.

Bereiter and Scardamalia. (2005). *Learning about writing from reading. Written Communication*, Vol1, No, 2, 163-188.

Bloom, Benjamin, et al.(1956). Taxonomy of educational objectives: The classification of educational goals. *Handbook I: The cognitive domain*. New York: David McKay Inc.

Blosser, P.E. (1995). *How to ask the right questions*. Arlington, Virginia: National Science Teachers Association.

Burns, Marilyn. (2003). The twelve most important things you can do to be a better math teacher. *Instructor*, April 2003, pp. 29-30.

Burns, Marilyn. (2005). Writing in math class? Absolutely! *Instructor*, April, 5.

California standards for the social sciences. (1998). California: California Department Education

California standards for the teaching profession.(1997). California: California Department of Education.

California Education Round Table Task Force on Mathematics Graduation Standards.(2007). *Mathematics standards for California high school graduates*. California: Intersegmental Committee of the Academic Senates.

Center for the Advancement of Learning. *Developing questioning skills, levels of questioning: An exercise*. (1998). Muskingum College: http://muskingum.edu/~cal/database/Question2.html, p. 1.

Center for the Advancement of Learning. (2006). *Questioning*. Muskingum College, http://muskingum.edu/~cal/database/questioning.html.

Charles, R. I. and Lester, F. K. (2005). *Problem-solving experiences in mathematics*. New Jersey: Dale Seymour Publications.

Chin, C. (2004). Questioning students in ways that encourage thinking. *Teaching Science*, 7, 4.

Clarke, David. (1997). *Constructive assessment in mathematics, Practical steps for classrooms*. Berkeley, California: Key Curriculum Press.

Constructivist views on the teaching and learning of mathematics. (2001). Virginia: The National Council of Teachers of Mathematics.

Cordi, K. (2009). *Unlocking the world of youth storytelling*. Retrieved on February 21, 2009. http: //www.youthstorytelling. com/teaching.html

Curriculum Development and Supplemental Materials Commission. (2000). *Mathematics framework for California public schools, kindergarten through grade twelve.* California: California Department of Education.

Davis, Robert B., Maher, C. A., and Noddings, N., et al. (1990). Suggestions for the improvement of mathematics education. *Journal for Research in Mathematics Education*, Monograph Number 4,

Davis, R. (1994). Say what: Getting students to ask questions. *The Language Teacher*, 18,7.

Davis, R. (2009). *ESL lab. Beyond the classroom walls.* Retrieved on January 40, 2009. http: www.esl-lab.com/research/question.htm.

Doyle, J. & Hogan, M. (2004). Theory application for online learning success. *Academic Exchange Quarterly*, Winter 2004, Volume 8, Issue 4.

DeBono, E. (1986). *Lateral thinking.* New York: Ward Lock Educational.

DeBono, E. (2007). *Lateral thinking and parallel thinking.* Retrieved January 30, 2009 www,edw.edwdebono.com.

Deming, E. (1993). *New economics for industry, government and economics.* New York: W.E. Publishing Group.

Eberle, B. *SCAMPER.* Retrieved on January 20, 2009. wwwfp. education.tas.gov.au/English/scamper.html.

Elstgeest, J.(1985). The right question at the right time. In W. Harlen (ED.), *Primary science: Taking the plunge.* Oxford: Heinemann.

Exline, J. (2000). *Science, technology and society.* Boston, Massachusetts: Houghton Mifflin,

Friere, P. (1970). *The psychology of the opressed.* New York: The Continuum Publishing Group.

Franklin Computer Dictionary. (2007).

Gilbert, S. (1992). Systematic questioning. *The Science Teacher*, 59, 9, 41-46.

Goldin, Gerald A., Davis, R. B., Maher, C. A., and Noddings, N. (2001). Epistemology, constructivism, and discovery learning in mathematics. *Journal for Research in Mathematics Education*, Monograph Number 4.

Golomb, Solomon. (1994). *Polyominoes in puzzles, patterns, problems, and packings.* Princeton, New Jersey: Princeton University Press.

Halliday, M. (1975). *Explorations in the functions of language.* London: Edward Arnold.

Harrell, W. (2009). *A perspective on inquiry.* Retrieved February 21, 2009. http://www.learnernc.org/lp

Harris, R. (1998). *Introduction to creative thinking.* Retrieved on January,20, 2009. www.virtualsalt.com.

Hervey, S. (2006). Who asks the questions. *Aussie Interactive,* August/September.

Holzman, David.(1991). Thinking skills score high marks. *Insight,* January 14, 1991.

Hyman, L. (2008). *Whatmit!* Linquistics Colloquium, London: Edward Arnold.

Hyman, R.T. (1979). *Strategic questioning.* Englewood Cliffs, New Jersey:Prentice Hall.

Intersegmental Committee of Academic Senates. (2007). *Statement on competencies in mathematics expected of entering college students.* California Intersegmental Committee of the Academic Senates.

Jakes, D. Pennington, M. and Knodle, H. (2009). *Using the internet to promote inquiry.* An epaper. Retrieved on January 21, 2009. http:wwwbiopoint.com/inquiry/ibr.html.

James, C. (2009). *Communication for the 21st century.* Retrieved February 12, 2009 http://www.speakercheewa,a,cm/ communication.html

Kasner, K. (1998). Would better questions enhance music learning. *Music Educators Journal,* 84, 4.

Kessen, William. (1986). *Developmental psychology.* Chicago, Illinois: World Book, Inc., Volume 5.

King, A. (1992). Facilitating elaborative learning through guided student generated questioning. *Educational Psychologist,* 27,1.

Koufetta, M.C. and Scaife, I. (2000). Teachers' questions types and significance in science education. *School Science Review,* 81, 296.

Kremer, Ron. (2007). *From crystals to kites and exploring three dimensions.* Palo Alto, California: Dale Seymour Publications.

Marzano, R. J., Pickering, D.J. and Pollack, J.E. (2001). Classrooms that work: *Research-based strategies for increasing student achievement*. Virginia: ACSD.

Mathematics framework for the California public schools. (2000). California: Department of Education.

Mavericks Teacher Resources. (2009). *Using inquiry-based learning*. Retrieved on January, 20, 2009. http: www.glenbow. org/mavericks/teacher/english/ingbl.html.

McKenzie, J. (2009). Telling questions and the search for insight. *Theory into Practice*, 7,1, November.

Mokros, J., Russell, S. J., and Economopoulos, K. (2005). *Beyond arithmetic*. Palo Alto, California: Dale Seymour Publications.

North American Council for Online Learning and the Partnership for 21st Century Skills. *Virtual schools and 21st century skills*. (2006). November.

National Council of Teachers of Mathematics. (2007). *Teaching children mathematics*.

Newby, D.E. (2005). *Higher level thinking*. Retrieved April 2007 from http: www.ehhs.cmich.edu/dnewby/questions.html.

Nikitina, S. and Mansilla, V. (2005).Three strategies for interdisciplinary science and math teaching. Project Zero: Harvard Graduate School of Education: *Goodworks Project Report Series, Number 1*.

Noddings, Nel, Davis, R. B., Maher, C. A., and Noddings, N. (2003). Constructivism in mathematics education. *Journal for Research in Mathematics Education*, Monograph Number 4, Virginia: The National Council of Teachers of Mathematics, Inc.

Operant conditioning, TIP: Theories, http://tip.psychology.org/ skinner.html. Osman and Hoffman. (1994).

Perfetti, C.A., Britt, M.A. and Georgi, M. (1995). *Text-based learning and reasoning: Studies in history*. Hillsdale, New Jersey: Erlbaum.

Pink, D. (2006). *A whole new mind: Why right -brainers will rule the future*. New York: Riverhead Press.

Polya, G. (1957). *How to solve it*. Princeton: Princeton University Press.

Questioning and research on questioning in the classroom. (2000). Salmon River and GLC Eisenhower Project, www. potsdam.edu/EDUC/GLC/ike/quest.html.

Ratway, B. (2009). *Social studies education*. Retrieved January 20, 2009. Dpi.wi.gov/calsocstudies.html.

Repo, Allen. (2008). *Interdisciplinary research: Process and theory*. London: Sage Publications.

Roseberry, C. (1990). *Increasing the language skills of children from low income backgrounds: Practical strategies for professionals*. New York: Plural Pub Inc.

Rowan, Thomas E. and Robles, Joseph. (1998). Using questions to help children build mathematical power. *Teaching Children Mathematics*, May.

Rowe, M.B. (1987). Using wait time to stimulate inquiry. In W.W. Wilen (Ed.) *Questioning techniques for effective teaching*. Washington D.C.: National Education Association.

Rubinson, F. (2002). Lessons learned from implementing problem-solving teams in urban high schools. *Journal of Educational and Psychological Consultation*, 13, 3.

Salmon-River Eisenhower Project. (2003). *Questioning: Research on questioning in the classroom*. GLC Eisenhower Project. Retrieved on January 10, 2008, www.potsdam Edu/EDUC/ GLC/ike/quest.html

Sandora et al. (1999). A comparison of two discussion strategies on students' comprehension and interpretation of complex literature. *Journal of Reading Psychology*, 20-177-212

Schank, R.C. (2009). The right answer. *Engines for Education*. Retrieved on January 30, 2009. http://www.engines4ed.org.

Schmoker, Mike. (1999). Results and the key to continuous school improvement. Alexandria, Virginia: Association for Supervision and Curriculum Development.

Schrock, C. (2000). Problem solving: What is it. *Journal of School Improvement*, 1,2. Fall/Winter.

Steffe, Leslie P, Davis, R. B., Maher, C. A., and Noddings, N. (1990). On the knowledge of mathematics. *Journal for Research in Mathematics Education*, Monograph Number 4, Constructivist views on the teaching and learning of mathematics. Virginia: The National Council of Teachers of Mathematics, Inc.

Stenmark, Jean. (1989). *Assessment alternatives in mathematics: An overview of assessment techniques that promote learning*. University of California, Berkeley: California, California Mathematics Council and EQUALS.

Taba, H. and Inlow, L. (2004). In W. Searles, A taxonomic study of curriculum development models used in science education. *International Journal of Science Education*, 3.

Tobin, K. (1987). The role of wait time in higher cognitive level learning. *Review of Education Research*, 57, 1,69-95.

Traina, Richard P. (1999). What makes a good teacher? *Education Week on the Web*, www.edweek.org.

Ventriglia, L. (2009). *Best practices interdisciplinary vocabulary: The rule of 3*. Sacramento: YounglightEducate..

Wallerstein, N. (1983). *Language and culture conflict problem posing in the ESL classroom*. Reading, Massachuetts: Addison Wesley.

Warner, M. and Leonard, J. (2004). An emergent problem-based course for middle grade teachers. *Middle School Journal*, March.

Wassermann, S. (1994). *Introduction to case method teaching: A guide to the galaxy*. New York: Columbia University Teachers College.

Wesch, M. (2008). Inspiring good questions and anti teaching. *DMU Exchange*, December.

Wetzel, D. (2008). A common question for students learning algebra, geometry, Trigonometry. *Science Teaching Tips*, August.

Wetzel, D. (2008). *Twenty questions children ask*. Retrieved January 30, 2009. http://homeschooling.suite101.com/article.

Wilen, W.W. (2004). *Questioning techniques for effective teaching*. Washington D.C.: National Education Association.

Wiles, J. and Bondi, J. (2001). *The new American middle school: Educating preadolescents in a period of change*. Columbus, Ohio: Merrill Prentice Hall.

Wirtz, Robert W. (1976). Banking on problem solving in elementary school. Washington D.C.: Curriculum Development Associates, Inc.

Zhang, J. and Mo, R. (2007). Reconsider Confucius' enlightening reflection: Implications on heuristic teaching. Sino-US English Teaching, 4,7.

Zemmelman, S., Daniels, H. and Hyde, A.(1993). Constructivist teaching and Learning. SSTA Research Centre Report, 97,7.

About the Author

Linda Ventriglia is the Director of the Center for Teaching Excellence. Linda Ventriglia has a Ph.D. in Curriculum and Instruction and a Masters in Public Administration from Claremont University and Harvard University. She also completed three years postdoctoral research at Harvard in second language acquisition and literacy development. A former teacher and school psychologist, Dr. Ventriglia has served as an educational consultant across the United States and internationally. She has also served as Chief Consultant to the California State Legislature on the Education and Workforce subcommittee. Dr. Ventriglia is the author of *Conversations of Miguel and Maria: How Children Learn a Second Language* (Pearson), *Ready for English* (McGraw-Hill), *Santillana Intensive English* (Santillana U.S.A. Publisher) and *Teaching Strategies for the 21st Century*, and the *Best Practices in Education Series and CDs and videos*. Dr. Ventriglia has received a number of grants and has done national and international research on effective learning strategies. Dr. Ventriglia has also written a number of articles and has been featured in articles in educational journals including the *California Educator, The CTA Journal*.